SWEEPER KEEPER

TOMMY LAWRENCE

PETER KENNY JONES

SWEEPER KEEPER

TOMMY LAWRENCE

The Story of
Liverpool and Scotland's Legendary
Flying Pig

Foreword by Ian Callaghan

pitch

First published by Pitch Publishing, 2024

Pitch Publishing
9 Donnington Park,
85 Birdham Road,
Chichester,
West Sussex,
PO20 7AJ
www.pitchpublishing.co.uk
info@pitchpublishing.co.uk

A CIP catalogue record is available for this book from the British Library.

ISBN 978 1 80150 694 6

Typesetting and origination by Pitch Publishing

Printed and bound in Great Britain by TJ Books, Padstow

Contents

Dedicated to Thomas Johnstone Lawrence

Born: 1940, Dailly, Ayrshire, Scotland.

Died: 2018, Warrington, Cheshire, England.

Acknowledgements

IT'S ALWAYS a daunting task trying to ensure that everyone who has helped with this mammoth project is correctly thanked and there are so many people that deserve a mention. So, in an attempt to cover all bases, if you're not mentioned below and very well should be – then I'm sorry, and thanks for helping make this reality.

First, I should start with Jeff Goulding. A fellow author and Liverpool fanatic, Jeff was originally approached to write this book and I can only apologise to everyone reading who thinks he would have done a better job! Although I probably agree too, I hope that Tommy's story has been left in good enough hands with myself!

If you're looking for the next book to read, then I would wholeheartedly recommend: *The Lost Shankly Boy: George Scott's Anfield Journey*; *The Untouchables: Anfield's Band of Brothers*; *Stanley Park Story: Life, Love and the Merseyside Derby*; *Red Odyssey: Liverpool FC 1892–2017*; *We Conquered All of Europe: Red Odyssey II*; and *Champions Under Lockdown*,

Red Odyssey III: Jürgen and the Holy Grail – they all just so happen to be written by Jeff too!

Next up comes Stephen and Jayne Lawrence and Tracey Murray, the children of Tommy, and it's their burning love for their dad that made this book a reality. Most people grow up thinking their father is a superhero and to keep this mystique throughout your life shows that he must have done a pretty good job. For many reading this, Tommy Lawrence is a famous Liverpool goalkeeper, but for Stephen, Jayne and Tracey – he's Dad. Their help in making this possible was priceless, and through their own tales and contacts this book has taken the shape that it's left in for you to read now. A massive thanks to them for allowing me the honour and responsibility of this task and I really hope that it does justice to your dad and everything you wanted to achieve by honouring his life.

Speaking of dads, I really couldn't have done this without mine! Aptly also named Tommy, for this project my dad has been a godsend for this and everything I do. With my middle name being Kenny, it's not hard to see where the love for football and Liverpool FC comes from. Stories from his younger days of following the Reds around the country and across the continent made me appreciate the times that came before my birth in 1994. This love for football and LFC means that this third book of mine is now a reality. My dad deserves a co-author title and a split of the royalties because of all the hard work he does for and with me. Thanks for everything you do for me in life and for your tireless efforts again with this.

Annie, my soon-to-be wife. It's so exciting that we're both able to pursue and push our own interests and careers and both have each other's backs. It's never a doubting word but pure encouragement from each of us to help the other thrive. We work so well together and I can't wait to see where our lives take us. As long as we're together, there's no stopping us – thanks for always being there for me.

Mum, you should be here to enjoy everything that we're all doing and I'm so sorry you're not. Without being able to read any of my books, or attend the book launches, or any of the multitude of things you would have done at the drop of the hat to support me in this and my life – I'm still benefitting from everything you did for me. Your advice is still audible in my head and I can still feel you holding my hand through it all. Thank you and we all still miss you so much.

Rebecca, Thomas, Laura, Gray and bump – thanks for being there for me whenever needed. Whether it's as a second set of parents, to let me look after the dogs and the house, to let me drive you to the airport for Venezuela or for the constant support – I thank you all.

Steve, Netty and Joe – although the Dunning family library wasn't needed as much for this book, I appreciate your support for everything I do. Although we are already, I'm looking forward to being officially family soon and couldn't ask for a better group of in-laws!

Farrell Keeling, Rick Elliott, Ste Carson – the WhatsApp group of support, always there for me whenever needed and the help you all provide in different ways for any request is amazing. The Empire of the Kop lads in Liam Togher and Max Rudd too; your support in the last book was brilliant and it's great to be able to call you both colleagues. Only because you ask for a thanks every time, here it is: Tony Gore, Paul Shaw, Pab, Libby, Jack and Dan!

Then there's the Seed City squad, Doc Johnson and all the lads and girls who are always there for me whether it be book related or otherwise – I really appreciate all your support: Tom Helowicz, Ailish Taulty, Jay Sharples, Freya Wright (soon to be Sharples!), Jonny Allen, Lauren Davies, Ryan Irvine, Lucy Flynn, Chris Nugent, Jack Baguley (again), Hope Bradbury, Dan Mythen (again), Meg Evans, Warren McCann, James Lee-Hindle, Sam Walker, Mike Campbell, Jake Atkin, Peter Robinson, Joe McConnell, Abie Price (and Sofia!), Katie Hooker, Adam Gilbert, Tom Gaunt, Tom Yardley and hopefully that's everyone this time!

Wider family of Jackie White, Ed Jones, all my aunties, uncles and cousins, all of Annie's family who travel to book launches and support me too (especially Terry and Claire's mammoth effort for the last book launch!). It's very humbling to know the support I have from you all and there's too many to mention, but I really do appreciate you all. Genuine supporters of my work like Rena Liddell, Phil Mason, Karl Reynolds, Chris Hesketh, Elizabeth Piert, Carol Prescott, Alex Olajos, Paul Dunning, Shawn Perry, Jayne Nel, Barry Rogers, Caitlin Stephenson, Chris Yates, Liam Holden, Mike Greensmith, Mike Nolan, Graham Strickland, Joanne O'Leary, Rob Storry, Pritchards Bookshop, Murdoch Kennedy and many more!

Jonny Stokkeland was a massive help with his personal archive of information. His database was invaluable and the records and statistics at the end of the book are mostly from his work. Gudmundur Magnusson provided information on Tommy's team-mates and opponents throughout his career, which was again invaluable. Charlotte Sargeant from the BBC, who helped me track down Stuart Flinders for his help. Andrea Granagan, Ian Rigby, John Hutchinson, Dave Evans, Moira Hughes, Jodie Jones, Gary Locke, Ray Montgomerie, Dean Nelson, Joanne Harney, Sheridan Smith, Kellie Boersma, Bunny Melia, Sonia Waltho, Rob O'Brien and Jarek Zajac, who helped me track down several of Tommy's former team-mates and opponents. Chet Murarji, Michael Makison and Terry Waller, for help with research and images to be used. Everyone above was selfless in their support of helping make this book possible and every gesture is hugely appreciated.

The interviewees: Mary Bailey, Stan Boardman, Phil Boersma, Ian Callaghan, Roy Evans, Trevor Farrington, Doug Fraser, Howard Gayle, Eric Grundy Snr, Eric Grundy Jnr, Brad Heenan, Mike Henshall, Liz Hoare, David Hunt, Julie Hunt, Dick Johnson, John Kaye, Chris Lawler, Steve Lawrence, Adam Lawrence, Scott Lawrence, Kevin Lewis, Ray Mathias, Frank McLintock, Gordon Milne, Ryan Murray, Tracey Murray, Dale Roberts, George Scott, Willie Stevenson, Jimmy Tarbuck, Bobby Thomson, Gordon Wallace, Paul White and Jack Whitham. Everyone helped make this the story it is, and whether it was a five-minute chat or several hours, the words have all been vital to ensure this is interesting, true to life and full of tales that nobody has heard before.

Jane Camillin, Duncan Olner and Alex Daley from Pitch Publishing, who work so hard behind the scenes to make all of this possible and believed in me once again to write a third book with them.

It really is impossible to thank everyone and I hope you don't feel let down to not see your own name in here. I want to pass a genuine heartfelt thank you to everyone above, everyone forgotten and mainly to the reader. There's plenty of people in my life whose support is massively appreciated, but for my work to reach anyone who doesn't know me on a personal level and then to see and be sent support is humbling. Although the stories of other people is the main reason anyone wants to read, to support anything I've done enough to spend your own hard-earned money is mind-blowing and I hope you appreciate how thankful I truly am.

About the Author

THIS IS my third book and, firstly, thanks so much for being interested in reading the story that's about to follow. I'm under no illusions that it's the life of Tommy Lawrence that will attract the majority of readers and not the name of the author, but it's an absolute honour to be given the responsibility to tell his story.

However, if you would like to know more about me, then here's your chance! I'm a football historian, author and writer and have been involved in writing about football since I graduated from Liverpool Hope University in 2017. Studying history gave me the opportunity to delve into football at the end of my undergraduate degree in 2016, where I looked at the love for football on Merseyside during the interwar period. This expanded when I completed my master's degree the following year and looked into the similarities and differences between Bill Shankly and Harry Catterick during their respective reigns at Liverpool and Everton.

The end of university brought with it an idea to first chop up my two dissertations and approach Liverpool and Everton fan sites, before broadening my experience with new articles being written. I then pushed myself to look further afield than clubs with an L postcode, and that led to opportunities writing about new and interesting topics. I then pushed to be published in magazines and programmes, leading to opportunities at English Football League clubs before Liverpool agreed to let me write for them. Paid writing opportunities soon followed and I'll forever be grateful to Tapas Iyer, who offered a first regular paid job.

David Cottrell, the former editor for Liverpool FC programmes and magazines, then inspired me to approach publishers about writing my first book. *Liddell at One Hundred: A Family Portrait of a Liverpool Icon* was published in 2021, and soon before it was released I was successful in my application to work for Empire of the Kop as a full-time writer. This led to a realisation of a dream of working as a writer, even more amazing as it was (and still is) all about Liverpool. My second book, *Crossing the Park: The Men Who Dared to Play for Both Liverpool and Everton*, was published in April 2023 and allowed me to repeat my university studies by looking at the relationship between Reds and Blues.

As a football fan, I'm as fanatical about Liverpool FC as I think it's possible to be – from having my middle name inspired by Sir Kenny Dalglish, to being mascot for the club in 2003 and now not missing a home match (Covid breaks aside) at Anfield since March 2011. Trips around the country and Europe have been some of the highlights of my life, with Gini Wijnaldum's second goal against Barcelona being an unrivalled moment in my many happy memories as a fan.

To be able to tie together a love for football, an appreciation of history and a desire to ensure that the role of important, influential and unique individuals' lives are both remembered and appreciated all means that it's truly a pleasure to say that at the age of 29 all of the above has been achieved.

Now, this is another huge step into being able to continue my love for all the above, through the life of Tommy Lawrence. The responsibility of this task, tied with a love for doing it and the unique opportunity to meet and speak with so many bastions of Liverpool's history for this truly special period, is a huge honour.

I hope you enjoy learning, reminiscing and reading what's to follow in this book and hopefully for what's to come in the future.

Thank you for taking the time and I hope to hear your thoughts on the book one day.

Pete

‘I Played in It’ – 2015 BBC Interview

IT’S NORMAL to begin a book about the life of one man at their birth. Perhaps when discussing a footballer it could open on their debut appearance, but here it’s a little bit different. Tommy Lawrence has a reputation among a certain era of Liverpool supporters for being one of the greatest goalkeepers in the club’s illustrious history and the stopper during a time that’s storied for being the transition from Second Division strugglers to Bill Shankly’s all-conquering heroes.

However, the passing of time has led to some younger and newer fans not even knowing the name of the legendary ‘Flying Pig’, nor what he achieved in his 390 first-team appearances. Instead of being interested in his winner’s medals and Scotland caps, awareness of the goalkeeper boils down to a clip less than 30 seconds long.

For those who aren’t aware yet, in February 2015, BBC North West presenter Stuart Flinders was in the right place at the right time. Speaking on the show, the reporter described the event: ‘It’s a moment that struck a chord here, throughout

Europe and further afield. You can read about it in German or Russian, Polish or Vietnamese. I was in Liverpool to record what we call a "vox pop", interviewing members of the public completely at random about a specific Liverpool and Everton match and I got more than I bargained for.'

He certainly did, and the full transcript of the meeting that was soon shared around the world is:

Flinders: 'I'm just wondering whether you remember the derby match in 1967 at Goodison, FA Cup fifth round and it was shown on a big screen at Anfield at the same time, do you remember it?'

Lawrence: 'That's right, I do – I played in it!'

Flinders: 'Did you?'

Lawrence: 'I was the goalkeeper for Liverpool!'

Flinders: 'Really?'

Lawrence: 'Yeah!'

Flinders: 'Well, that's a stroke of luck me meeting you. Sorry, can you remind me of your name please?'

Lawrence: 'Tommy Lawrence.'

Flinders: 'Tommy, nice to meet you. What do you remember about it?'

Lawrence: 'It was a great game, yes. Alan Ball scored the winner.'

Flinders: 'He did indeed.'

Lawrence: 'Yeah, he did, yeah.'

And that was it, 27 seconds of footage that shot the

name of Tommy Lawrence right back into the limelight. The video went viral and, as Stuart Flinders described, it was translated and dubbed into nearly every language imaginable, with it seemingly being shared and reposted every few months still today. At the time it came out, Tommy's niece lived over in the Middle East, in Qatar, and she first discovered the interview when it appeared on her television translated into Arabic!

One video on YouTube, at the time of writing, has 11 million views, but the number of times it's been uploaded and shared on different accounts and different websites means it's been watched much more than that. It's a remarkable sensation but the main reason for it being so widely appreciated are the facts that you don't need to be a football fan to understand it, the pride on Tommy's face to be given the chance to speak about his playing days and how humble he was throughout.

Many big egos would have scoffed at the idea of not being remembered, even people with half of the footballing CV that Bill Shankly's former No.1 had. Instead, though, the then 74-year-old patiently waited for an opportunity to state that he was part of the match and that's what makes the video so popular. It also makes it the perfect place to start the story of his life as there aren't many better ways to view what type of person Tommy was than by watching a clip that's less than half a minute long.

Seeing as this is a book about Tommy Lawrence, though, and that this video may well be the reason why many people have either decided to read this far, or are even aware of his existence, it makes sense to delve a little further. To do this we need to take a short trip to Everton. The reason for crossing the park is to analyse the role of the only other man mentioned in the legendary clip – Alan Ball.

'The name of Alan Ball, made up of only eight letters, has become one of the biggest in British football. Indeed, it is a name that has to be considered when talking about the best players in the world.'

These words were written in 1969 by Harry Catterick, the manager who brought Alan Ball to Goodison Park. Ball arrived from Blackpool shortly after helping England claim the 1966 World Cup, and his record-breaking arrival on Merseyside made him one of the biggest attractions in the First Division. There was plenty of excitement around the man coined the 'human fireball' already, but when the fifth round of the FA Cup drew together a Merseyside derby consisting of the reigning champions on the red side of the city and the cup holders from the blue half of the city, it was always going to be a memorable clash.

March 1967 will forever be remembered for this meeting and one that's safe to be forever held as one of the most important between the city's two clubs. In what was possibly the biggest Merseyside derby ever, the teams met at Goodison Park. What made this meeting extra special was the decision to also broadcast the tie at Anfield on giant screens to allow as many people as possible the opportunity to watch it live. This being the days before Sky Sports and a television in every home meant it was a revolutionary idea by ABC Television that doubled the audience for the match. Indeed, it was the first-ever live relay on closed-circuit TV of an FA Cup tie, with eight giant screens measuring 40ft x 30ft and costing £115,000 each being erected on the pitch.

Within three hours of tickets going on sale at both stadiums, every one of the available 105,000 were sold. Extra police presence had to be called upon to control the huge crowds that gathered. Around 100 people at Goodison Park had to receive medical attention because of the frantic scramble to be able to witness history, as queues stretched round Walton Lane. This not only shows the thirst for football within the city during this time but also how successful both teams were and why there were interviews taking place about the match nearly 50 years later.

As Tommy said, Alan Ball scored the only goal in an Everton victory and endeared himself to his new fans. The new Blue scored four times past Lawrence in Merseyside derbies and went on to have great success against the Reds in terms of finding the back of the net, but arguably none were more important than this one.

It was a wild and stormy night that certainly wasn't ideal for the state-of-the-art screens at Anfield, and it also hindered the ability for either team to get any real rhythm in the match. *The Guardian* described referee Kevin Howley as 'extravagantly tolerant' for not sending anyone off, despite the tackling being as savage as the weather. Although Bill Shankly claimed that the result was a 'travesty of justice', the home team were dominant on the evening and deserved their place in the next round.

Ryan Murray shared his memories of what he had been told by his grandad, Tommy Lawrence, about the interview and the match:

> He remembered people, remembered faces, remembered scorelines, it's ridiculous. In the very famous video of him that goes viral, he remembered the scoreline of that, but then also he went home and didn't tell anyone that he got interviewed by the BBC and everyone found out while watching *North West Tonight*.
>
> There's so much more to that story that no one knows beyond the interview itself. My grandad didn't usually travel beyond the Warrington area, especially when he was that age. I think he went to do something with LFCTV in Liverpool and then he was walking through the city centre and got stopped by the journalist.

He thought it was a wind-up because the cameraman was shaking when he got asked the question. In his eyes, he thinks the cameraman knew that he was a footballer. And then when he replied, you can see it kind of lights up in his eyes when he realises, it wasn't a joke.

He said he thought it was a joke until the guy asked for his name and then the cameraman was shaking, there was a whole sort of emotion around it where the journalist was kind of red in the face and said he's never seen someone look so embarrassed.

He knew who scored the goal in it, even also added that it was a great finish. He was always adding that extra thing for you, he would say it was a great finish (even if it was a deflection).

But then that was it. He went home, he didn't tell anyone, he didn't say anything. And from what I was told, they were sitting down for TV like they always do with their dinner and he appears on TV, and his wife turns to him and goes: 'You didn't tell me you got interviewed today,' and he said, 'Oh yeah, the BBC interviewed me,' and he had no understanding of how viral it went.

I woke up the next day and saw that my grandad was trending on Twitter and I tried to explain it to him. The only way I could explain to him what had

> happened was that Katie Price was trending number two and he knew who Katie Price was. He was like: 'Oh, I beat Katie Price!' That's all he was saying around it because he had no idea what Twitter was, how it worked or what trending was!
>
> There was some follow-up to the interview as well. The BBC came and did another interview with him in his home and then with my Uncle Ste [Tommy's son].
>
> I really like that story because I think it really captures that humbleness, yet incredible detail and memory. But then also, he was a guy in a world that he doesn't really know, and he never knew how big he was or has been since the late 60s.

There were so many friends and family members that couldn't help but bring the famous interview up during our chats, and the overriding conclusion was, as team-mate for the famous match Willie Stevenson said, 'That's typical Tommy.' The way in which he didn't try to embarrass Stuart Flinders for not knowing who he was, how happy he was to talk about football, the perfect recall of the match and how humble he was to not bring it up with family and friends afterwards.

This humility and glint in the eye was not only the reason that it went viral but also why Tommy was back in the limelight again. His career was relevant once more to a much wider audience, and even if the former goalkeeper didn't realise it, the influx of messages to his friends and family members reinstated a feeling of pride. Whereas some names are lost in time, it was another opportunity to say: 'That man from the interview on the BBC – that's my dad/grandad/uncle!'

Perhaps to finish in the words of Gordon Milne, another player from the match against Everton, would be the best conclusion to this chapter:

> That bloody television interview he did, that depicted him perfectly, didn't it? They say that went viral or whatever it does today. I don't know what they say, but you couldn't paint a better picture of Tommy's character than that bloody interview.
>
> It was him as a human; some people would be offended by being asked. In that team there were strong personalities, Big Ron [Yeats] and the Saint [Ian St John] had strong personalities and they would react differently to how Tommy would react, or Chris Lawler. They'd all react in different ways but that was the mix we had at Liverpool. You can't have 11 people the same, you've got to have a mixture that works.
>
> He just came across in that interview as absolutely bloody fantastic. The great thing about that was that I had so many people who talked to me and to my wife about it that weren't really interested in football,

didn't know who Tommy Lawrence was, but how can someone who played in the cup final, won the cup final, be just like talking to the guy next door?

It was absolutely brilliant. You could just say have a look at that interview, and thousands upon millions have watched it, that he was just a lovely man who finished his career with not much more than his medals and memories.

That's how it was in those days. The players didn't get enough money to save enough money, to finish the game in any other way. But it showed Tommy's character, personality, ability and humility, and just that he is a great, great guy.

Preface

TOMMY LAWRENCE is a man who's footballing achievements are nowhere near as appreciated as they should be. Had it not been for a viral video clip being repeatedly shared online, then many today wouldn't even know who he is. In many ways a chance run-in during his later life has superseded the fact that he won the First Division twice with Liverpool and was a crucial part of the first-ever team to win the FA Cup for the club.

By speaking with those who knew him best inside and outside of football, we can begin to understand how his legacy should be much more than 'that old bloke the BBC ran into for the famous interview'. When so many different people from different walks of life have nothing but good things to say about a man, it shows that they also deserved to be remembered for much more than what they achieved during their working life.

Thankfully, though, Tommy's working life brings with it masses of exciting tales. Being at the epicentre of Bill Shankly's

Liverpool revolution means that the stories and matches of this time all so heavily feature the Scotland international. Not only did he play in these storied matches but he was also a pioneer in his position, widely being regarded as the first 'sweeper keeper'.

This talent of playing the ball out from the back and being adept at coming off his line set the South Ayrshire-born stopper aside from his peers. When we look at the expected standards of goalkeepers in the modern game too, it's safe to say that Tommy could have easily transitioned to life in the Premier League era. Doing this in a time when it certainly wasn't expected of a man who stood between the sticks and was allowed to pick up back passes from his own team-mates means that his and Shankly's revolutionary talents were often misunderstood by his contemporary supporters at Anfield.

Despite the many highs achieved in the eight seasons he was Liverpool's No.1, falling so painfully short of being the main man for ten years meant that a testimonial wasn't on offer to him. Players in the modern era rarely stay at a club long enough to be rewarded with such an event, but in the 1960s, in which Tommy played the vast majority of his top-tier football, they were much more commonplace. However, it wasn't the lack of fanfare and appreciation that cost the father of three most – it was the lack of financial stability he was able to receive because of missing out on this.

Hard times fell on the man who spent the latter seasons of his career with Tranmere and Chorley, times that affected his family life and how he would spend his final years. Although the football stories and BBC interview may be why many want to pick this book from the shelves and learn more about the affectionately named 'Flying Pig', you may soon discover that it's the life away from football and the stories that haven't been heard before that are the most immersive and interesting, about a character that had much more to him than saving shots in Shankly's goal.

By the end of his story you'll see that Tommy Lawrence was a fantastic goalkeeper and a brilliant man, but also so much more than that. If his interview has been the first step of learning about the man who famously lost the plinth to the FA Cup in 1965, then buckle up for a bumpy ride of highs, lows and everything in between.

Foreword

Ian Callaghan
Liverpool FC 1960–1978
380 appearances with Tommy Lawrence

TOM WAS a good friend as well as a team-mate. He was fearless, he would just come out and get the ball off people's feet, not thinking about the consequences of getting kicked! He was a fearless goalkeeper and a very, very good goalkeeper too. Tommy Lawrence was the most friendly guy, he never got upset and very rarely did you see him lose his temper.

I became friendly with Tom and Roger Hunt because they were from the same village. I used to go to Culcheth, where they were from, and I wasn't a golfer but I would walk around with Tommy and Roger; it was great. I would walk around the golf course, chatting and having a laugh. It was great because, if anything, they were the two that I got really close to in the Liverpool team. Tommy was just such a lovely guy. I got to know Tommy's dad too, and went to see his family often. He became a very good friend.

When we played at Melwood in training, Tommy loved to play out and he was a good player too. I know he's a goalkeeper but he was a good outfield player in the five-a-sides. He was probably one of the first sweeper keepers as well. Tommy was like a one-off, everybody just regarded him as a terrific keeper.

He was up there with the best I played with. Ray Clemence was an absolutely fantastic goalkeeper and Gordon Banks has to be the best, but Tommy was up there with them at the very top as a keeper.

He was such a nice guy and that's why I was friends with him. Tommy was always nice with people, you can't say more than that about him. It was great to be a friend of his and I'm fortunate enough to say I was.

Testimonials

Adam Lawrence – Grandson

He was very quiet about who he was, he wouldn't want loads of publicity, he was always in the background and didn't seek too much drama, like some of the pros do these days.

Bobby Thomson – Liverpool team-mate

He had everything that you'd want in a goalkeeper. He commanded his 18-yard line completely. He'd be shouting here, shouting there, a smashing fella. You couldn't find a bad word to say about him, he was always laughing.

Chris Lawler – Liverpool team-mate

I got on well with Tommy. He was an easy-going, nice fella. He was more of a friend in the end. I don't think people realise how good he was, but he learned a lot, and he taught Ray Clemence a lot too.

Dale Roberts – Family

He was a big man, not a big character, a big man with a soft heart. Lovely soft heart for a lovely man, without question.

David Hunt – Roger Hunt's son

Tommy and my dad were thick as thieves.

Dick Johnson – Tranmere team-mate

I can honestly say this: he was genuinely the nicest man in football that I ever met.

Eric Grundy Jnr – Family friend

I remember him being a very generous person and a very sporty person. He was a nice man and he was really, really generous.

Eric Grundy Snr – Family friend

He was very jovial, a good bit of fun. We had a way of having fun together; we would always have good craic.

George Scott – Liverpool team-mate

He never seemed to be nervous, took everything in his stride, very confident. Became a big, big part of the team and is sadly missed by everybody who knew him.

Gordon Milne – Liverpool team-mate

He was there at the beginning of it all at Liverpool and it was a privilege to play with somebody like Tommy.

Gordon Wallace – Liverpool team-mate

I would say he was brave, a great stopper, fearless. I think 'the flying pig' describes it. People might say about his stature but he used to be able to fly around that goal – tremendous.

Howard Gayle – Liverpool

That era, some would call the side 'Shankly's men', but Tommy's one of the gods to me. They were the reason why we are where we are today. They were the building blocks, the first ones who set the standards for the rest of us to follow. We should forever be appreciative of them.

Ian Callaghan – Liverpool team-mate

We had a fantastic team in the 60s and you just felt great, with a great bunch of lads who got on well together and the trophies kept coming. When you have got a team like that and you're all friends and get on well, I think it shows on the pitch.

Jack Whitham – Liverpool team-mate

I found him a lovely man, Tommy, a very friendly guy.

Jimmy Tarbuck – Friend and comedian

He was just a reliable nice man. He wasn't a screamer or a shouter. The lads all liked him at the back. He was sound.

John Kaye – Scunthorpe United and West Bromwich Albion opponent

He played like a sweeper, and he didn't have to make many saves because they were so clever playing at the back, he was fantastic. I think he could have played outside, anyway, as a defender; he was so good at reading things.

Julie Hunt – Roger Hunt's daughter

I do remember a very close friendship with Dad and Tommy. They were boyhood friends, and it was funny how their lives intertwined as they did.

Kevin Lewis – Liverpool team-mate

I would say he was up there with the best goalkeepers in the country at that stage. In terms of playing and maintaining the goal for us, he was brilliant for that. He was a strong lad, you could go up for the ball with him, go up for crosses, and he would knock your head off, so we couldn't mess about!

Liz Hoare – Liverpool fan

He was just superb, he was brilliant.

Mary Bailey – Sister

I just remember him always being there. He was very modest but friendly and very accommodating to people, anybody who wanted any help, he was always there.

Mike Henshall – Daten FC

What a pleasure it was to know the man. He was just such a lovely, lovely chap.

Paul White – Founder of Tommy Lawrence's fan club

He was a great person, funny. Whenever he used to come to ours, he'd always say to my mum: 'Mrs White, have you got the scones ready?' She'd always be making him scones every time she knew he was coming up, and what he didn't eat, he'd take with him!

Phil Boersma – Liverpool team-mate

The most amicable, generous piss-taker! Him and Roger [Hunt] were just fucking total banter-takers, piss-takers all the time! That was what it was all about.

Ray Mathias – Tranmere team-mate

Tommy was a very down-to-earth fella when he came from Liverpool. After all the achievements, he was just another person, and that's the way he treated everybody else as well – with respect.

Roy Evans – Liverpool team-mate

You have to have a great goalkeeper and, at the end of the day, I'd say it's not always about the great saves you make, it's about the whole thing that you do as a goalkeeper. You've also got to make them great saves and he was good at that, even though he wasn't the biggest lad in terms of height as a goalkeeper. He was a great keeper for us.

Ryan Murray – Grandson

You'd sit down and listen to him, even if it was the same story, you'd listen to it because he was so captivating in the way he said it and he'd use voices. Like mimicking Bill Shankly in a kind of scary headmaster kind of tone. The whole thing with him was always around the storytelling.

Scott Lawrence – Grandson

He just loved the interaction with fans, not just Liverpool fans, even Evertonians would come over and say hello to him, ask him how he was doing. His face would always light up.

Stan Boardman – Liverpool team-mate and comedian

Tommy was always covered in shit because he'd be diving all over the place! His green sweater was black because the pitches then were not green like they are now, they were just mud. If he had a day where he was covered in shit and he'd have to get in the bathroom, we all tried to get in the bath before Tommy Lawrence because he was always caked in mud!

Steve Lawrence – Son

He is one of the nicest men you will have ever met. Loved talking about football, loved football. Very proud man from where he came from in Scotland, he loved going back to where he was born in Scotland too. He's a proud man and loved talking about football and just enjoyed people.

Tracey Murray – Daughter

I'm so proud. I don't worry at all about saying, 'My dad's Tommy Lawrence,' not because I want anything from it but I want to talk about him. I want his memory to carry on. I want people to hear his stories. I want them to remember him.

Trevor Farrington – Daten FC

There was no standoffishness about him. There was no air of superiority about him. He was very humble-natured and just quiet and unassuming. Yet get him on a football pitch and you couldn't shut him up! He was a different beast on the football pitch.

Willie Stevenson – Liverpool team-mate

He was great. I wouldn't say he was one of the best kickers of the ball, but I'll tell you, when it came to saves … and what's the keeper there for? Save, stop the ball going in his goal. He couldn't care less as long as he stopped it from going in – which he did.

Growing Up

THE PHRASE 'humble beginnings' is often overused, but when it comes to the Lawrence family during Tommy's childhood in South Ayrshire it's certainly true. One of three children to Francis (known as Frank) and Robina (known as Ruby), William (known as Billy) was the eldest, his sister Mary the youngest child and the family were packed into a small cottage. The home had one bedroom and one living room, with two inset beds in the wall of the living area. This was to house five people at its most cramped and was also the place that both Tommy and his sister were born.

The family home had no running water, so trips to the stream at the bottom of the garden that fed off the Water of Girvan was the only way the Lawrences could collect some for their daily needs. Acres of green land surrounded them, and the main village had little more than a shop, a pub and a small local football team. The cottage actually belonged to Ruby's parents, Thomas a miner and Mary, names she would use for two of her own children. While Frank was part of the war effort and after Thomas passed away in 1942, the two mothers could help each other in more ways than one.

The village of Dailly was as humble as the Lawrence family home but that didn't stop Tommy from being a normal, active, sporty and popular child within the local community. Seeing the young Scot without a ball at his feet (not just in his hands!) was as likely as seeing running water in the family home. His popularity may have also been down to the fact that he was the person who could provide the football for their daily kickabouts. It does always seem that these infatuations with the sport start very early when it comes to anyone with a future in the game, and that's again the case here.

It's also impossible to not mention the impact that the Second World War had on Tommy's childhood. Being born during the fighting would have obviously been a traumatic experience, more so for his mother than the second infant child she had to care for. As Frank was also part of the fighting, it made it all the more stressful for Ruby. Being in the Royal Electrical and Mechanical Engineers, his ability to understand and repair the more sophisticated technology involved in the war effort made Frank a crucial part of the British Army unit and led to a trip to Sierra Leone as part of his duties. Helping to teach the locals how to drive was an insight into his passion for mechanics and the positive impact the Scot had on most people around him.

Frank and his three brothers all saw action and miraculously all made it back home. The first time Tommy actually met his father was as a four-year-old, once the war came to an end and the world had returned to (relative) peace once again. It's a story that's certainly not out of the ordinary for anyone born in the early 1940s, but a sobering reminder of the impact this must have had on so many families.

Tommy and his elder brother Billy were three years apart in age but had a very close childhood in wartime and post-war Dailly. Their younger sister Mary was born over five years after Tommy, so for much of the very early days in the future Scotland international's life his brother was his best friend. Both went to the same school and would spend a lot of time together before, during and after their days in different classrooms.

Tommy was always proud of his big brother and there's perhaps no better story that illustrates this than when the pair visited the local harbour when they were younger. As five-year-old Tommy was playing near one of the ropes that was mooring a ship, he tripped and fell into the water. Thankfully, Billy was on the scene, and despite being just three years older, he made the quick decision to dive in and save Tommy from a certain death by drowning. No matter what shenanigans Billy was to cause in later life, he always had a keen and vocal supporter in Tommy. It would be commonplace to hear him say, 'Don't you say that about my brother, he saved my life!'

Once Frank had settled back into life in Dailly, and before Mary was old enough to join her elder brothers at school, the family made the short move to Ayr in search of their own family home and to allow Ruby's mother some respite from three small children in her overcrowded cottage. Tommy's parents were looking to restart their lives after the war and create opportunities for their three young children.

When Ruby first met her future husband, she was working as a parlour maid in service, and by the time the war commenced she was a housekeeper with much of the same roles being handed to her. She would work all day maintaining someone else's home, to then go back and help manage her own. Frank was a chauffeur before he left for the army and his interest in cars had led to an increased understanding and interest in how they worked. It was then the plan that, once he returned from the war, the job search would commence in the more densely populated Ayr as a motor mechanic, given his experience during the conflict.

Once Frank could find a job, he could then try to get the family a home, which came in the form of a prefab council house. After a lot of hard work, stress and time apart, the Lawrence family finally had a place that the five of them could call their own.

This terrific work ethic and strong desire to better themselves and the future of their children meant that Frank and Ruby were about to make a decision that would change the course of the life of their family. Having experience working with cars meant that the former soldier always kept an eye and ear out for any potential opportunities to work on and drive in the type of cars he could simply not afford to own himself. Although fixing them was certainly a passion, it never compared to the thrill of sitting in the driving seat. When the news came round that a reasonably wealthy company owner, Adam Lythgoe, was in need of a chauffeur, it caught Frank's attention. Hearing that they were also interested in finding a new housekeeper and that the roles came with a tied house too made it almost a no-brainer. Both he and his wife could work for the same family together, be provided a new home, and they had experience in the exact roles on offer. There was one stumbling block though – the jobs were over 200 miles away.

Once Frank posed the idea of a move to Culcheth in Warrington, the town based right between Liverpool and Manchester, it took some convincing to uproot the entire family and their lives. Seeing as both of Ruby's parents had now passed away though, the only family she had left in the area was her brother – another Thomas. The move was eventually agreed upon in 1954 and it was to be a decision that certainly made the future possibility of Liverpool finding themselves a new goalkeeper much easier, given Tommy's move to the North West of England as a 14-year-old.

The children arrived in a new village and had a tough task of settling in, with their 'strange' accents making them immediately different. Tommy's love for sport and ability meant that it was perhaps easiest for him to adapt in Culcheth Secondary Modern. Mary attended the local grammar school, and it was always a topic of constant teasing from Tommy, whether out of jealousy or not; it was a running joke within the family. This joking spirit and sporting talent makes it easy to understand why he found his new surroundings so easy to settle into.

This wasn't just in football though; Tommy represented his school in athletics, he was a great sprinter, and a keen and able table tennis player, where his talents were honed on the makeshift table erected by Frank in the family backyard. Tommy would take on his whole family, and his desire to win at all costs meant that the rest had to improve quickly to keep up with him! This grew into an interest in tennis too, but football was always his first love.

This sporting acumen may have also stemmed from the long walk that was needed to get to class. Tommy's daughter Tracey remembered stories from her dad: 'He used to say that he used to walk five miles to school. He didn't, it was probably more like two. But I know there were no shoes and he used to walk across the fields just to get to the school. Him and my Uncle Billy, they would walk off in the morning on their own, all across the fields from Dailly to school. They used to play out in the fields afterwards too. It was hard but he only had good memories, he always spoke fondly of those times – he loved it.'

It wasn't just cars that had the interest of Frank either – there was also a strong passion for football from him. Being a promising player in his younger days meant he was always interested in the sport, although the war commencing in his early 20s curtailed any hope of progressing in the game. His love for Ayr United was passed down to his two sons, although this passion was somewhat transferred to Bolton Wanderers when the family moved south.

The two young brothers were now in a new area and their father was keen to help them flex their footballing prowess. Whether this was an attempt to live vicariously through his children due to his lost playing days, or a genuine certainty in their talents, Frank's belief in the boys would soon pay off. The presence of two other local brothers around the same age as the Lawrences meant that there was also company for them whenever Tommy brought his ball along for a kickabout. These were Peter and Roger Hunt. Anyone who recognises the latter brother's name will certainly be interested in seeing his first mention in this tale, but for anyone unaware, you'll soon be hearing a lot more about him!

Frank would often use his contacts and personability to pitch the services of his sons to local teams, which was a tactic that would soon lead to the ultimate reward. Before

Tommy had his growth spurt though, the feedback would often be to bring the youngster back once he had grown a bit more – something that didn't happen until around his 16th birthday. It wasn't just between the sticks that you would see the future keeper playing, however, as most of his youth was spent pursuing a role as an outfield player.

Back to family life, Frank's parents were both still alive and thus provided the Lawrence family an excuse to travel back annually to Scotland and also visit whenever they had the opportunity. William Lawrence can probably be attributed some credit for the sporting life his grandson Tommy was going to have but certainly not for his soon-to-come rather uncomplimentary nickname of 'The Flying Pig'. William was a horse groomer and a jockey, and his passion for the sport meant that well into his 70s he worked in the racing stable in Ayr, showing the equestrian's love for horses. For a profession where being short and light is the desired profile, it's almost comical to learn that Tommy is often best remembered for being a footballer whose physique was closer to the man stood in the crowd behind him than it was to the 21 athletes in front!

There's also a distant family link to Joe Corrigan, a man who went on to play in goal for Manchester City for 13 years and work as a goalkeeping coach for Liverpool for ten years. It seemed that this athletic prowess was always going to come to the fore at some point and Tommy certainly seems to have made the most out of the sporting gene present in the Lawrence family tree.

This inherited ability was shining brightest in Tommy and these trips back to Ayr meant that he maintained an appreciation and love for Scotland, despite leaving at such a young age and never moving back to the country of his birth. Not just through his teenage life but throughout the later years too, he returned to the cottage where he spent the first nine years of his life, which was something that reminded the soon-to-be star of how far he had come. The sacrifices of his parents not only moved the young Scot closer to the footballing institution he was soon to join but also allowed him an opportunity to begin his own working life too.

When he left school at 15, Tommy was looking to earn himself a wage to help the family, and to spread his own wings in adult life. This once again came through the same family that his parents worked for, in an office working as a clerk on Hob Hey Lane for Joseph Lythgoe, son of the man who had provided Tommy's parents with their employment in Culcheth. This was enough to hand the teenager his first step on the working ladder, while he continued to play football at a local level for Stockton Heath (today known as Warrington Town) in the mid-1950s.

Speaking about growing up with her elder brother, Mary Bailey said: 'I don't think Tommy ever really changed at all. He was one of these people that didn't think *if*, it was always *when*. He didn't doubt that he could do anything, like when he went for his driving test and he never thought, *If I pass* …, it was always, *When I pass* … He didn't doubt himself. He was always pretty confident when he was young, confident in his own ability. He obviously didn't mind being the centre of attention. You've got to be like that or you couldn't do what he went on to do.'

This rather interesting childhood of moving homes certainly moulded Tommy into the character he later became. His father Frank had a passion for cars and his grandfather William for horse racing, and although neither rose to the level of stardom that Tommy was to experience, these strong male examples of following dreams and earning a living from them would have certainly provided a young aspiring footballer with confidence that there was a chance to excel in his own passions. This tied in with his dad being so positive about the youngster's ability on the pitch and created a perfect platform from which to go on and achieve great things. Being constantly reminded of his humble start in a tiny cottage provided an appreciation of what hard work can lead to. By being one of the lucky families that didn't experience huge loss during the Second World War also meant that positive role models were a constant presence in Tommy's childhood.

When the Lawrences returned to the original family home in Dailly in 2023, the sight of a St Helens-born Evertonian living there was a great shock. The way in which the building has been renovated, but still keeping much of its original charm, is something that would be sure to have brought a huge smile to Tommy's face – someone who was very proud of where he came from. Cherry-picking the best parts of each aspect of his childhood meant that he made the most of every opportunity his family worked so hard to provide.

From the generosity of his grandmother, Mary, to allow them into her cottage, to the sporting prowess of his grandfather, William; the tireless work ethic of Ruby, to the ingenuity and positivity of Frank. The community spirit of Dailly and Culcheth and his own morals and natural abilities all created the perfect storm, which sprouted a 15-year-old on to the cusp of greatness.

Stockton Heath to Liverpool

FRANK LAWRENCE had a few contacts in his little black book and he had already tried most of them in an attempt to get Tommy out of the office and into senior football at the top level. Other than the details of a manager who was transitioning from Grimsby Town to Workington and to Huddersfield Town within two years, a man named Bill Shankly, Frank didn't have the details of too many others within the game.

Tommy was performing well for Stockton Heath and Frank penned letters to many clubs in the local area in the hope a scout could come to watch his son play. With Billy reaching his late teens, it seemed as though the only chance for the Lawrences to make a name in football was through the youngster who had decided that his long-term career now lay as a goalkeeper. Tracey recalled stories her dad would tell her about his father: 'My dad used to say that he was hard on him. On a Sunday, my grandad would have took him off to play football and they came home and my nana would be making the Sunday dinner. She'd say, "How did he play, Frank?" If it wasn't that good, he'd say, "Like a bloody big Jessie!" I think he was quite hard on him.'

After a year juggling working as an office clerk and performing for Stockton Heath, the long-awaited growth spurt finally came for a now 16-year-old Tommy. Trials at football clubs had undergone a relatively new reform and there was a much more proactive approach to dealing with the hundreds of requests that would come in the post. In 1952 at Liverpool, manager Don Welsh set aside a month's block of trials during pre-season, where two sessions per week would be put on for around 30–40 teens to be put through their paces. It was a great opportunity for the youngsters to work first-hand with some senior coaches from the world of football, including those from Anfield. The likes of Tom Bush, Jimmy McInnes, Albert Shelley, Jimmy Seddon and Jack Balmer would represent the Reds but other Lancashire-based scouts were also invited, with a view to helping as many talented teenagers as possible to find the opportunity to find a club. Although Liverpool would get first refusal in these particular sessions, Everton were doing similar within the city, and many other clubs followed around the country.

After witnessing the successes of 'homegrown' talents such as Billy Liddell and Bob Paisley, who had arrived for nominal fees and would go on to be mainstays of the team for many years, it seemed the club was making an effort to try to build a new team on a shoestring budget. It was a great plan, but as the Reds were relegated to the Second Division just two years later, perhaps it was something that was introduced a bit too late.

Nevertheless, these trial sessions were exactly what Frank knew Tommy needed, and after several rejections due to an ironically small stature, things were changing. With it now being 1957, an improved physical standing for the budding goalkeeper was enough to inspire a father's continued ambitions to push for more trials. The details of Tom Bush were all that Frank needed to have another attempt, and this one was different.

Frank joined his son on the train journey from Culcheth to Melwood training ground in West Derby, where two sessions a week were offered as an opportunity to impress. Tommy took it with both hands (literally), and after impressing Bush and the other youth coaches, it was decided that the young Scot could continue to train twice a week. This led to an opportunity for word to spread to new manager Phil Taylor, and it was agreed that Tommy would be part of Liverpool, full-time, in the youth set-up.

Little did Taylor know but his A, B and C teams, the place for youngsters to earn their stripes within the club, had many of the players who would go on to form Bill Shankly's all-conquering squad. For anyone unaware, youth players in those days would be given the goal of working their way from C, to B, to A, to reserves, then to the first team. If the club saw promise in a player, it would make them part of the ground staff and would often offer housing to anyone travelling from further afield. Given Tommy's office job and relative locality to Liverpool, this wasn't on offer to him.

Alongside some of the future stars he was sharing a pitch with, Tommy was also rubbing shoulders with several young men who were set to make their name in fields other than football. One such man was Stan Boardman, who was also signed by Liverpool in 1957 and went on to spend two seasons in the youth teams. This was, of course, the same period as Tommy, and the man who went on to make his name as a comedian shared his football memories:

> I got to Liverpool for the trial and I went to Melwood and met all these fellas; Johnny Morrissey, Alan Banks, Bobby Campbell, Lenny Ashurst, Frankie Twist, Phil Ferns. There was some good lads there who never made it but Tommy was always our goalkeeper. We were all youngsters, all under 20.
>
> I always remember him being in the A team, B team, C team – he came right through the lot but I thought he was a pig farmer from Warrington the way he talked! I used to call him the pig farmer, but he was always laughing, always smiling, I never had a bad moment with him.

One day, I'm sitting with Lenny in the bath, and he said, 'I'm going to Sunderland, you'll never get a game here because all the old men in the first team and the reserves, they don't want us young ones playing because they won't get their wages.' We were only on £15-a-week then, and were a Second Division side full of older players, clinging on to their career as they needed the money. The younger lads had no chance of forcing our way in.

The funny thing about the Melwood baths was that you had about six people in one bath and the water was black as the ace of spades! You used to sit at one end and we would try and get in as quick as you can to get clean water, bloody freezing cold as well. It was all wooden, it was like wood huts. It was like a cottage, woody type, you know, wooden steps going in and all that. We'd jump out the bath as quick as we could and then run to the team sheet to see if you were in the squad; Tommy's name would always be on there.

Tommy always had a big green shirt; goalkeepers always wore green in them days. When you play with the A team or the B team, you always had different players and they were always trying things out. So, you never knew which side you would be in but our paths crossed a lot and I was with Tommy for most of my games.

Tommy was always covered in shit because he'd be diving all over the place. His green sweater was black because the pitches then were not like they are green now, they were just mud. If he had a day where he was getting a bit kicked at, he would be covered in shit and he'd have to get in the bathroom. So, I tried to get in the bath before Tommy Lawrence because he was always caked in mud!

Them days we didn't have the boots that they have today, they had knock-in studs. That was another disadvantage, knock-in studs, leather, big heavy ones – laces and shin pads were massive, some people used to put books down there because they couldn't afford the shin pads! They'd stick an atlas down there! Bob Paisley would be there and Tom Bush, they used to run the A team and the B team, Paisley would coach. All we ever did was run, we never got any coaching how to pass the ball, how to do anything. We just ran right around the perimeter of Melwood, run, run, run, run, run, run, run, lap after lap, after lap, and nobody ever told us to go and pass anywhere or do anything like that.

I used to play centre-forward and Tommy was a good kicker of the ball out of the penalty area, although the ball in them days could never go over the halfway line. They were too heavy, especially when they were wet, and I would get the brunt of it. Sometimes you went for a header and your brain would go blank and then two minutes later you're back heading it again – the ball was so heavy.

It was a tough skill being a goalkeeper. They wouldn't really tackle because they had their eye on the ball and a lot of these centre-forwards, like me, would look at them and go for keepers rather than the ball. It was a cutthroat game, but you have to try to work to your strengths. You'd go up and you'd knock them off the ball, so they wouldn't be able to get it.

We all trained Monday and Tuesday, worked through the week, and if we weren't playing when the first team were, or you're injured, we'd get a ticket in the band box at Anfield. All young lads, turning up in our respective work uniforms, playing footy, living the dream and hoping of getting a career in the game.

You can only imagine the fun the young lads had together and it certainly seemed like a brilliant time to be at the club. However, there were some glaring issues within Liverpool in the mid-to-late 1950s. The facilities were not up to scratch and much of the club needed a real facelift. An ageing playing squad with a somewhat understandably selfish outlook on clinging on to their careers because of the much-needed wages, meant the standards were slipping.

Coaching was little more than running around a pitch, and manager Phil Taylor had barely any say or influence over a board that seemed devoid of ambition to make a change. Boardman even revealed a later meeting with Taylor, long after the pair had finished their football careers, where it was revealed that even if the manager liked the look of some of the clearly talented younger players within the A, B and C teams, he wasn't allowed to select them. The board would present the manager with the team he had to play, and this explains the slump from First Division contenders for the title to Second Division mediocrity.

This meant that, although it was an undoubtedly exciting time for any youngster at Melwood, it was also one where many would understandably contemplate their future. Tommy was different from the likes of Boardman though, as he had been given a glimpse of a promising career ahead. On six occasions in the 1957/58 season, Lawrence had started for the reserves and, by the end of the campaign, was competing with Doug Rudham for a place in goal. Seeing as Rudham was the club's main No.1 just two seasons earlier and played for the first team on two occasions in the same season, Tommy had fought his way into contention, which was more than a promising start to his career as a Red. Competing with Rudham was a badge of honour, as the South African international was 32 years old when Tommy's maiden campaign with the club came to an end. It was soon announced in the *Liverpool Echo*:

> Anfield Signing – Tommy Lawrence, a 17-years-old goalkeeper from Warrington, who has been on Liverpool's amateur staff for 12 months, was to-day signed on full-time professional forms. Hitherto Liverpool have had only two professional custodians, and this move brings up their strength to normal for the goalkeeping position. Lawrence who is 5f. 11ins. And 12 stone, has been playing exceptionally well in the 'A' team.

It was agreed that Tommy would remain third choice for 1958/59, and he did so behind two men who had represented their countries and were in latter stages of their careers but still very able to perform at a high standard. To learn from these experienced professionals was a huge help to the young man still taking the train twice a week from Warrington, and their actions as mentors was something that would be replicated by their protégé in later life.

Now that Tommy had a strong case to make that he was competing for the starting role in Phil Taylor's second team when his second full season at the club came to an end, there was a route to the first team. The 19-year-old had 29-year-old Tommy Younger firmly within sight in the coming years. The Scotland international was another positive impact on the younger Tommy within Melwood. The club's current No.1 at this point was a real fan favourite and had proved a dependable option between the sticks. By the end of the 1958/59 season, he had featured in a whopping 120 of a possible 126 league matches over the past three years.

It was agreed that Tommy Lawrence would remain at the club for the upcoming campaign, entering the 1960s, and he would again fight with Rudham for a place in the reserves, with the long-term aim still being to displace Younger in the first team. However, Phil Taylor's goalkeeping options were now not as they had at first appeared. It was reported by the *Daily Mirror* in June 1959:

> Liverpool's giant Scottish international 'keeper, Tommy Younger, left the club yesterday to go back home as player-manager of Falkirk.
>
> In return Liverpool get the Scottish club's Under-23 International Bert Slater.
>
> The deal – a straight swap – was one of the best kept Soccer secrets for years. Even Younger had no idea of a transfer when he was called to meet manager Phil Taylor yesterday.
>
> Last night he said: 'It came as a complete surprise. I didn't want to leave Anfield. But I thought it was up to me to look after my future.'

It seemed somewhat underhand to replace the much-loved Younger and move for a 23-year-old with experience (albeit at youth level) for the same nation that Tommy hadn't yet managed to break into. This transfer would have set alarm bells ringing for Tommy. His ever-welcoming route to the first team had been hugely hampered, and if the club had faith that it would be Lawrence wearing the No.1 jersey for years to come, surely they wouldn't have pushed for the arrival of Bert Slater.

It seemed very much that Liverpool wanted Slater to be the man to guard their goal for the coming years, and if they had to force out Younger to do so, they were willing. The one remarkable fact about their new stopper, though, was that he stood at just over 5ft 8in, which is far below the average height of a Premier League goalkeeper today at well clear of the 6ft mark. Add in the fact that this was the era where the man in goal could be virtually assaulted by oncoming attackers, his height was a big concern. There was no doubting the talents of the new man, and Tommy's concerns when hearing the news of his new competitor for the dream role he had at the club were real, but when he first locked eyes with Slater, these worries must have shrunk a little.

Winger Kevin Lewis described Slater: 'Bert was a good goalkeeper; he would dive at people's feet. He was chirpy, he wasn't quiet – he was a good lad. Bert was very agile and all over the place, in a good way, but he was small compared to Tommy. Bert was probably a little bit too small for a goalkeeper.'

So, initial worries may have started to ease when Tommy met Slater for the first time. All eyes were on the new man in goal when the start of the season's campaign began against Cardiff City. It was never in Tommy's nature to be anything but a terrific team-mate to those around him, and his awareness of the need to be patient was abundantly clear. However, a lesser man may have hoped that a trip to Wales for the first match of the season would end in criticism for the new man in goal. The *Liverpool Echo* wrote:

> From this criticism must be excepted the Scottish debutant goalkeeper, Slater. In no way could he be associated with the defeat. A less capable player would have been beaten more frequently and if Slater can go on improving on this standard Liverpool's worries in goal appear to have been taken care of for many years to come …
>
> But on the credit side were numerous saves, brought about by his remarkable agility, and his spectacular pounces to the extreme ends of his goal did him the greatest credit. What roars of delights would feats such as he achieved produced from an Anfield crowd. He is a worthy successor to Tommy Younger and, unless I am very much mistaken, will prove not only as spectacular as his predecessor but every bit as successful.

It was far from the report that any team-mate who had hoped ill upon someone they were competing with in the long term would want to read. This was a great start to Slater's career as a Red, and when he stepped on to the pitch for his third match, a second at Anfield, many thought they had unearthed a hidden gem and no doubt were lauding the decision to trade in Younger for a new model. Yet the *Liverpool Daily Post* described this match against Hull City by stating:

> Slater palmed upwards and over his head into the net one of Coates' efforts and when Metcalfe scored with a lob from the wing the ball curved gently over the goalkeeper's outstretched arms and over the line, leaving spectator and player alike speechless.
>
> In the circumstances Liverpool did well to get [the victory] in a match which they might well have found themselves losing everything through those goalkeeping mistakes. Slater is quick and good when dealing with low shots, but his lack of inches and the fact that he was facing the strong glare of the sun made him particularly susceptible to any ball coming in high.

This disastrous day in front of his new home supporters was nearly costly in terms of points dropped for Liverpool but was more damaging for Slater personally, as this was enough for Taylor and the team selectors to drop the new man into the reserves and reinstate Doug Rudham to the first team. The 33-year-old proved to be a steady pair of hands but a run of four wins in the following 13 matches meant that the uncertainty around the team led to more squad changes. Several rolls of the dice were made in the shape of veteran club legend Billy Liddell being reinstated from the reserves, youngster and fellow Culcheth resident Roger Hunt being handed his first match for Liverpool, and another change in goal, with Slater set to come back in for Rudham. Some changes worked, some didn't, but it screamed of desperation from those in charge.

The club's last league title had been back in 1947, the first campaign after the Second World War, and they hadn't reached any higher than eighth in the seven years after this success. Then 1954 saw the Reds handed the indignity of relegation to the Second Division, somewhere they hadn't visited since 1905, in a campaign where they immediately bounced back to the top tier at the first time of asking. Never had Liverpool spent more than a solitary season in the Second Division as they had bounced straight back up on three prior occasions, but this time things would be very different. Finishing 11th in the second tier in 1955 was the lowest the club has ever finished, and despite Taylor's subsequent attempts to achieve promotion seeing Liverpool finishing no lower than fourth, he couldn't crack the code.

Finishing in the top two guaranteed promotion and was the only aim as each season began, but Taylor's fourth attempt in 1959/60 felt very much like his last chance. Defeat to Lincoln City left the Reds in 11th after 17 matches. The man who played nearly 350 times for the club he went on to captain still holds the record as being the only manager to have never overseen a Liverpool match in the top division, and it was revealed by the *Daily Mail* in November 1959:

> Phil Taylor resigned yesterday after 23 years with Liverpool as player, coach and team boss. I hesitate to call him manager – his official title for the last four years – for he never had complete charge of the team.
>
> And I suggest that it was this lack of authority that finally drove him to walk out of Anfield yesterday, admitting: 'I am tired. The strain of trying to win promotion has proved too much.'
>
> As gentlemanly as ever, the dapper Taylor, West Country accent undimmed by his long spell on Merseyside, refused to make any complaints. As he was never under contract, he was free to finish immediately.
>
> 'At Anfield I have never created any trouble,' he affirmed, 'and I am going out on that same note, for no one has ever caused me any trouble either.'

It was a classy exit from a respectable man who was little more than a scapegoat for a board of directors too scared to make the big decisions – it being telling that even Taylor's exit was even something they never orchestrated either. When Liverpool signed Tommy Leishman three days later, before a new manager was hired for the vacant role, he posed alongside secretary Jimmy McInnes, chief coach Reuben Bennett and Tom Bush – the man who Frank Lawrence had written to for Tommy's trial. This showed who was helping to make the footballing decisions at the club at this time.

Both McInnes and Bush were former players at Anfield, so were clearly pushing their opinions on what was happening on the pitch. Bennett and McInnes were also Scots, and with the new man who was set to walk into the manager's office being from the same nation, it was about to be a great time to be a Scottish Red, something Tommy was also soon to discover. The likes of Billy Liddell, Jimmy Harrower, new man Tommy Leishman and fellow stopper Bert Slater would have also welcomed the sight of Bill Shankly being handed the job as Liverpool's new manager.

Although Tommy was still some time away from his first-team debut, the way in which the club would propel itself from the Liverpool he was set to play for in a couple of years' time was beyond the imagination of the youngster still pushing for his first opportunity and of anyone attached to the club. With Rudham and Slater not instilling confidence in those currently in power, plus a swelling squad of aged players past their best and a dearth of talent in the younger age groups, what had looked a worrying situation for Tommy now appeared rosy. It was clear that Liverpool were on the brink of a revolution, and Shankly was about to deliver it.

Bill Shankly and Liverpool's Promotion from the Second Division

IT WAS ironic that when Bert Slater stood in goal for the first match of the 1959/60 season against Cardiff City, it seemed that a new era of Liverpool was about to begin. Victory meant that players, officials and supporters alike believed that this could be the season they finally exited the Second Division. Instead, when the Welsh outfit visited Anfield for their second meeting of the campaign, the Reds were about to lose 4-0 under the stewardship of the new manager Bill Shankly and belief in the club was at an all-time low.

As Slater picked the ball up for the fourth time from the back of his net and jeers met Shankly's new team, it was clear there was a long way to go before Liverpool had any chance of being promoted. Just as the fans had been wrong with their optimism after the first meeting with Cardiff, their despair after the second was as ill placed. As Chris Lawler stated: 'Shankly came and then it all changed.'

This is the story of Tommy Lawrence and it may seem somewhat unnecessary to delve too far into the character of his manager at this point, but purely in a way to show how he transformed Liverpool FC at this time and also impacted the life of all his players, this sidestep is needed. For a man that even Tommy admitted, 'When he first came, everyone thought he was mad,' he certainly made a big impact. It's unlikely many who have read this far will be wholly unaware of the legendary Scottish manager but this chapter will be dedicated to what he did for the club and his players during this momentous period.

It wasn't an immediate success but Shankly had a plan. He highlighted a list of 24 names of those he wanted to leave the club inside a year. The Scot wrote in his own autobiography that he believed Liverpool were 'overburdened' with too many substandard players. One of the men on his list was club legend Billy Liddell. The forward was so good at Anfield that for a lengthy period they were often coined 'Liddellpool'. Spending 22 years at the club and still being the oldest man to score for the Reds to date, with his 228th and final finish coming at the age of 38, it showed the new boss was ready to make the tough decisions.

He clearly had Tommy in his sights, with the goalkeeper sharing one comical story: 'He joined on the Saturday and on the Monday he came into the dressing room after the reserves had beaten Leeds 2-1 and said to me: "Son, I'm signing you as professional tomorrow." I said: "Mr Shankly, I've been one for two years.'"

Shankly also quickly had frictions with the board of directors. He described them as 'gamblers on a losing streak who were afraid to bet anymore'. This was somewhat understandable due to the 13 years they had gone without a trophy, and the six years they had spent in the Second Division. This complete gear shift from selecting the team for Phil Taylor to allowing someone with the talents but also confidence, brashness and ego of the Scot is, though, somewhat surprising. They couldn't have expected the 46-year-old would lay back and allow the hierarchy to dictate how he would manage the Reds and to restrict his ability to implement these decisive changes.

Nevertheless, it was a running theme of his tenure that Shankly and the board were often at loggerheads. The transfer fee of £13,000 paid for Albert Stubbins in 1946 was still the club's record amount spent on one player by the time 1960 came around. After clearing so much money from the wage bill by pushing for some of the elder statesmen to leave, it was time for investment. Despite strong performances after that Cardiff defeat, Liverpool were still not promoted come the end of the season. Although the hierarchy was impressed with a third-place finish, they were still uneasy about the idea of financially supporting all of their manager's big plans. In Shankly's first summer, though, he managed to convince them to finance some of his transfer wishes. Kevin Lewis was signed from Sheffield United for £13,000, Gordon Milne from Preston North End for £16,000 and Alf Arrowsmith from Ashton United for £1,250.

The manager's plans had been backed but 1960/61 was the same old story, the Reds missing out on promotion by six points and finishing third again. Ahead of the start of an eighth season in the Second Division, Shankly put two players at the top of his transfer wish list, but the board still met his desires with scepticism, stating that the club couldn't afford them. However, Eric Sawyer spoke up and said, 'We cannot afford not to buy them.'

Eric Sawyer had become a director at Liverpool in 1961 and is known as the financial brain behind the Shankly revolution. The man who joined after being director of Littlewoods Mail Order Stores for 30 years was key to the club's eventual resurgence in the 1960s. An accountant with a shrewd business brain, he was one of the few within the boardroom who shared the same vision as their new manager. With the club record fee now at the £16,000 spent on Milne, Sawyer was key in supporting Shankly's push to sign both of his main targets. These were Ron Yeats from Dundee United for £22,000 and Ian St John from Motherwell for £37,500. The likes of Willie Stevenson for £20,000 from Rangers and Peter Thompson for £37,000 from Preston North End were to follow within a year, and fortunes quickly prospered both on and off the pitch.

It cannot be underplayed just how bad it was at Anfield before Shankly arrived, Gordon Milne stating: 'Liverpool had been in the dumps, Everton were the team when I went to Liverpool, Everton were doing this and doing that, they had all the top players. Whereas Liverpool is in the Second Division, their ground's crap, the dressing rooms are crap, Liverpool were going nowhere. Shankly was just the beginning of it all.'

Given Shankly's ambitious dreams, had it not been for a vocal and powerful supporter of Sawyer in the boardroom, then what followed at Anfield simply wouldn't have happened. So, when it came to the arrival of Southampton to Anfield in April 1962, Liverpool needed a victory to ensure promotion, even with six matches still remaining of the season. One of the manager's first signings at the club, Kevin Lewis, was to be the hero, scoring twice on a memorable day. Speaking about the match, the Ellesmere Port-born forward said: 'The players were dancing around singing: "We've won the league", that kind of thing. You can't sort of explain, you're just part of a situation whereby you all played your part and you've got the result that you want – that's what it's all about really.'

Because of all that had come before, when Tommy Lawrence was finally handed his debut for the first team in 1962, Liverpool were a First Division club. Not only that, they had an entirely new playing squad too, and the presence of a 22-year-old starlet fighting his way through the ranks was perfect for Shankly.

* * *

In an effort to not repeat what was said before, this is the story of Tommy, but Bill Shankly is so crucial to it that we'll rejoin the story of our main protagonist in the next chapter. This seems like the perfect time, though, to provide some further context to why his manager is so important for this story. By speaking with many former players who were at the club during this era, there are several important themes that need to be shared to provide more insight and a different viewpoint into the events that follow in Tommy's career.

Monty Maclaren was a fellow young goalkeeper at the club during this time, and George Scott was a team-mate in the reserves, who retold one story that provides the wicked sense of humour his manager had:

> Big Monty never broke through, but he was about 6ft 6in, Monty, and he dropped a couple of shots, dropped a couple of crosses at Melwood and Shanks was watching. We were playing against Everton and we were two down at half-time and both had slipped through his hands, and Shanks comes into the dressing room looking for him.
>
> He says to him: 'Monty, son, you've got everything it takes – everything. You're big, you're

> hard, you're strong, you're fit, you're confident, you've got everything it takes … to make a bloody good policeman, son! You'll catch lots of crooks but unless you can catch a bloody football, you'll never make it as a goalkeeper!'
>
> The funny thing is, he became a policeman – he ended up being a policeman! That was just the sort of thing we used to get all the time.

Although it's a comical tale, it was a very clear message to a young goalkeeper that there were very high standards at Anfield, and in a very public message in front of all his team-mates stating that anyone who didn't meet them would be out the door. The delivery was perfect for a comedian but you can imagine it wouldn't be the nicest message for a player to hear about their own performance. The world was a different place in the 1960s compared to what we see today but all sportspeople need the competitive edge to make it to the top. Unfortunately for Maclaren, he didn't have what it takes to make it at Liverpool.

Although this may be an example of how Shankly could knock a player down if they weren't playing well, he was very talented at building his players up before a match too. Willie Stevenson revealed: 'He never shouted, he went around every individual player and maybe said a couple of words with them, but generally speaking he would say: "You're playing against a load of shite today. You will beat them five nothing!" and as far as he was concerned, we were going to win every game 4-0, or 5-0 and you couldn't persuade him from that.'

Gordon Wallace agreed when he explained how this happened in one match for him, against West Ham:

> Shanks was talking to me before the game and he wanted to talk with me about Bobby Moore. He says: 'This fella, he's captain of England but he can't kick with his left foot, can't kick it, take him down the left. Heading? He can't head the ball, son, can't head the ball, you'll beat him in the air all the time.'
>
> The game ended, I had done quite well, and I scored, and Shanks said: 'You've just played against the best player that England's ever produced – he's England's captain!' He made me feel ten feet tall and that's what he was like.

By taking the pressure off Wallace before the match, he had the confidence to go out and perform against a brilliant player in Bobby Moore. To then tell the young attacker afterwards how well he had played and how prestigious the calibre of opposition was just added to this confidence and self-belief even further. These tiny moments add the 0.1 per cent that's needed to help turn a good team into a great one and there's no doubt that man-management was Shankly's greatest asset.

Tommy himself recalled: 'He could convince an average player he's good, a good he's great. All week he's on about Liverpool's ability and in the dressing room it's: 'I've just seen Chelsea in the corridor, and they're a bunch of big girls.' You're up, them down, and you know you're believing it as much after five years as you did at the beginning. That's another thing about him – he never loses his grip on you.'

Despite so much praise being attributed to him for this period, though, there was one glaring belief that shone through from nearly every player who was able to provide help for telling this tale. Although Shankly was the figurehead and a man very much responsible for dragging the club from the Second Division into an all-conquering outfit, another person deserves a lot of credit. It's not a huge surprise to hear that the man who went on to win six First Division titles, three European Cups and five other major honours during his time as manager at Anfield was a hugely significant member of the coaching team – that man is, of course, Bob Paisley.

Kevin Lewis shared his thoughts on the coaching partnership of Shankly and Paisley:

> Shankly was forthright as a manager, but I would like to say that Bob Paisley was more of an influence on the boys. In training, in coaching, in getting us together and with the patting-on-the-back encouragement.

> Paisley was probably more important, I think, than Bill Shankly. Bill Shankly, he's got this character about him, he would just stand and watch you train. He had the five-a-side games, but the coaching was just sort of: 'Do a couple of laps.' You would only get the ball at five-a-side and Shanks would always pick his five or six – to make sure he won.
>
> So, he wasn't a man to put his arms around you, he wasn't like that really, but Bob Paisley was. He could deal with all the players. He was not hard, and if you've had a bad time, he could help you. But his coaching ability, and knowledge of other teams you were playing against, he was good at all that stuff, he was a good chap. If you think about it, we had Shankly, Paisley and Joe Fagan at that time. They all turned out to be good managers, it was amazing really.

It's hard to say that Paisley was underappreciated when he's widely regarded as one of the best managers in football history, but his role within Shankly's team is probably often ignored. There's no doubting what the Scottish manager did to take Liverpool from the Second Division and on to what was achieved, but football is very much a team game. Shankly himself would be the first to admit that he couldn't have done what he did without the team he had behind him.

Although Phil Taylor had perhaps been the personification of everything that was wrong with Liverpool at this time, more through his inability to have any real impact on what was happening on the pitch, the club was actually in a great position. An ageing squad, poor facilities and a board of unambitious directors – yes. But behind this was a hugely talented crop of youth players and some of the most gifted coaches in the history of the game.

It wasn't just Shankly who made the difference. Paisley succeeded him and his time with Liverpool spanned from being a player in 1939 up to retirement as manager in 1983. Joe Fagan was the next man in the top job at Anfield, and the Scouser arrived at the club in 1958, staying there until 1985. As well as this, Reuben Bennett had arrived the same year as Fagan and the Scottish former goalkeeper was possibly the closest ally of Shankly and was attached to the Reds until 1980. Then there's the likes of Ronnie Moran and Roy Evans, who were players at the time this dynasty began but also both went on to have crucial roles within the inner sanctum of Liverpool's fabled boot room. The 'boot room boys', as they were known, were not only immensely talented but were also all available to Shankly from the first day he walked through the entrance door.

This isn't to downplay the role of Shankly but to show that there's many contributing factors to what went so right for the Reds in the period that led up to Tommy Lawrence making his debut for the club and what followed in the 390 matches he played. When Frank Lawrence wrote his letter to Tom Bush asking for a trial for his son at Liverpool, he could scarcely have imagined what tremendous state the club would be in by the time Tommy was given his chance in the big time.

Life Outside of Football

FOOTBALLERS TODAY are seldom given the opportunity to be part of 'normal' society, their swelled wage packets and strict fitness regimes meaning they have little chance to interact with the average man on the street. Partner this with the extreme level of fandom in place in the modern era, then the image of two stars of the game sitting unbothered in a small local pub is almost unimaginable. That was the life of Tommy Lawrence and Roger Hunt in Culcheth though.

As was mentioned before, Tommy and his family moved to the small village of Culcheth, and what's a quite prosperous area of Warrington was perhaps most famous for one thing – Hunt Haulage. Originally established in 1929 by Richard and Harry Hunt, the depot was based on Church Lane, which was a literal stone's throw away from two things: the building Tommy and his future wife and children would call home and The Pack Horse pub.

There was certainly an affinity between Tommy and the pub in particular, where he would famously spend a lot of time. Local resident and family friend Eric Grundy Jnr recalled: 'Tommy liked to drink. He used to go to The Pack Horse, which was just around the corner. All sorts of footballers used to come down and drink there as well. I remember quite a few of the Liverpool players coming in and a few of the Manchester United squad coming too. I remember the Charlton brothers came once. They lived in Lymm at the time.'

The image of a small local pub welcoming some of the biggest stars in world football is astonishing. Add to this that they were also left relatively unbothered, and it's an almost unfathomable thought. Although Tommy and Roger being friends with fellow Liverpool and England team-mates and prestigious footballers in the North West wasn't an oddity, it must have been some sight for the locals! The pair weren't afraid to use their fame for good either, and several charity matches and events saw many of the game's biggest stars flocking to Culcheth to help out with important local causes.

It would be commonplace for Tommy's children to be sent into the pub to find their dad, under instructions from their mother Judy. They would go in, tell him to come home for tea and they would buy some blackjacks while waiting for the last drink to be finished off. Eric Jnr added:

> I had a younger sister and got sent out walking the baby while everybody watched Liverpool in the 1965 FA

> Cup Final against Leeds United. I remember walking around the village and thinking there's something wrong here, because the village was literally closed down – it was like a ghost town.
>
> That was my first recollection of how important Tommy and Roger were to the village. I don't think they were treated like celebrities and paid the sort of money that celebrities in football get today. But they had the respect of everyone in the village, both because of what they achieved and the respect to let them live their lives. The whole village pretty much became Liverpool fans because of them and probably still are today!

Despite the fact that there was a World Cup winner in Roger and a key part of the Liverpool team in Tommy, the pair were left to enjoy their lives in relative peace. With each major honour that came their way, particularly for Roger after England's World Cup success in 1966, the duo were approached for more and more autographs but nothing too intrusive. Because both men had grown up in the village, it was just part of normal life to have two celebrities being such a big part of the local area. They really were great friends on and off the pitch. The duo would not only drive each other to training but also to matches. However, Ian Callaghan explained one issue that came from the pair sharing cars:

> They were close obviously because they travelled together to games. One of the times the two of them were in the same car and they got stuck on the East Lancs Road and it got to a point where, there's no mobile phones obviously, I can't remember whoever it was but they were getting changed to step in for them. Tommy and Roger actually arrived about quarter to three or ten to three, got out the car and abandoned it outside and ran to the ground, and they just about made the game and both started the match!

Roger's daughter Julie shared the same tale, stating that Liverpool were fined £100 because of how late they arrived for the match. Julie shared another occurrence when the pair were caught in some more travel mishaps:

> There was another incident where they were travelling to a game in Leicester and they'd gone on the train and their other team-mates had gone direct from the club together. Tommy and my dad ended up getting stuck on this train, in heavy snow, for 12 hours and they were actually declared lost.
>
> My dad would always tell the story and say: 'We were stuck on this train together for 12 hours and there was no restaurant cart!' Can you imagine that happening today? So, they got to the ground finally

> and the game was postponed anyway because it was such bad weather, but you could just imagine them stuck in a car together, stuck in a train together. They must have had some adventures!

You would think that, after travelling together so often, the pair would get used to the possible congestion issues. Despite these two logistical nightmare journeys, it appears that even when they arrived on time there was some drama to be had! Coming into the team as a youngster in the mid-60s, Phil Boersma explains how the comical bickering between the Culcheth couple was the normal start to most days:

> Tommy, I can't say enough about how great he was. He used to come in every morning and there would be a story from him and Sir Roger. Whenever they got in to training there was always a drama because Tommy couldn't fucking drive! Roger didn't want to drive either, though, so it would be the same thing every day. Roger would come walking in and say, 'Someone give us a fucking drink!' They were like Morecambe and Wise when they were together, the banter was just so funny. They're only up the road in Warrington and made out like they'd been driving for hours. Roger would say, 'I'm risking my life here with Tommy.' He said, 'He must have got his driving licence from

> the supermarket!' Oh, they were hilarious together – hilarious!

The constant bickering was seemingly all a comical cover-up for just how much the two men loved and respected each other. Another tale from Julie Hunt centred around the day that Roger broke Liverpool's scoring record, with his 242nd effort taking him above Gordon Hodgson:

> In the 1968/69 season, my dad had broken the Liverpool goalscoring record held by Gordon Hodgson. The game was at Chelsea and my dad was disappointed he'd not got the record on home soil. The players and Chelsea FC gave them the match ball, and so on the way home on the train they were all in a celebratory mood. Tommy then borrowed this ball and it soon went missing on the train. Tommy had this reputation, probably because he lost the FA Cup plinth [we'll get to this later!], for losing things, so my dad was a bit concerned that he might never see this ball again!
>
> All the way through this journey home his heart sank as he thought he was never going to see the ball again. They finally got back to Liverpool and at the station Tommy just tapped him on the shoulder. Dad turned round and Tommy said, 'Here you go,

> here's the ball!' and he was absolutely thrilled because he thought he'd lost it. That ball was treasured all his life and there was no way Tommy would have lost it on him!
>
> They had a friendship that endured from growing up, into their football, careers and long after it they were still friends, which is really, really special.

Roger's son David recalled being sat in the backseat with his mother while Tommy and his dad drove them to matches at Anfield. Listening to two huge football stars being nonchalant about the prospect of performing in front of tens of thousands of supporters was the norm and set up the sons of both men to play together for local club Daten FC.

Roger's brother Peter played football locally too, starring for Stockton Heath, which was the club where Tommy started his senior football experience. Plenty of locals used to claim that they thought Peter was better than Roger when the pair were growing up but it's safe to say that one had a much more prestigious career than the other! Peter went on to be a big part of the family haulage business.

Tommy was originally more Peter Hunt's friend as the pair were in the same school year in Culcheth. As there was only 18 months between the Hunt brothers, they were always together away from school – mostly playing football. They all played together for Croft, another village just outside

Culcheth, and would get changed in a little shed behind the goal on Croft playing fields, alongside Johnny Green, who went on to play for Tranmere, Blackpool and Port Vale. It was here that Roger's talents were spotted by Stockton Heath Albion, the team today known as Warrington Town.

Roger was excelling but wanted his mate and brother in the same team, so he recommended them both, but this was at a time when Tommy had decided he had a career as a striker, not a goalkeeper. Both Roger and Tommy would, of course, go on to shine brightest, and their lives were destined for bigger and better things at Anfield together. However, it was these early days that they all spent together, where they were nothing more than football-obsessed youths with aspirations no higher than kicking a ball against walls in the streets of Culcheth, that forged their bond and love for the game.

Tommy and Roger had such a strong friendship that their interactions on the pitch improved. Jimmy Tarbuck, a comedian who Shankly invited to come and spend time with his players on matchdays, recalled messages they would give each other in the dressing room before matches: 'Roger would say, "Tom, I might drift to the right there," or "Aim one up there, I'll get it." They would work little things like that.' This understanding came after many years of friendship and being team-mates for so long.

The Lawrence family as a whole were part of the community of Culcheth too. Tommy's parents lived on

Wigshaw Lane and he lived with them up to the age of 23 when he got married. So, the man with 35 first-team appearances for Shankly's team would finally fly the nest. For that first season in the big time and the years before in the reserves, he would return home and share a bedroom with his brother Billy. Eventually they both moved out, and Billy, wife Joan, their daughter Fiona and dog Cindy were on Bollin Close (after they moved from living above the Post Office). Billy was a local truck driver and his wife Joan a shop assistant. Although the pair weren't wealthy, it shows the relative normality of footballers' wages at this time as they lived very close to Tommy. Next door to Billy was the Grundy family, and Tommy lived with his wife and three children on Avon Road.

All this was in the vicinity of the Hunt Haulage depot and The Pack Horse. Everything was so close, including Daten Football Club and the social club there, which was near where Mary lived on Warrington Road. Roger lived two minutes away on Culcheth Hall Drive; to quote Tommy's daughter Tracey: 'the posh part' of the village! Even Leigh Golf Club was less than a five-minute drive. Without knowing the landscape of Culcheth, this all just shows how close everything Tommy needed was. The only reason to travel was to play and train for Liverpool, which was certainly worth the effort!

Although Tommy's life wasn't any better than anyone else living in Culcheth and the wages the players were on in these days were nowhere near as substantial as we see in the game today, he still enjoyed a comfortable lifestyle. It wasn't as if he needed to be looking for shifts in The Pack Horse to make up his wages. Tommy's son Steve remembered Christmas days being full of 'sacks and sacks of toys'. It was a happy family life while Tommy was at his pomp, and none of them wanted for anything.

Tommy's wages were substantial enough to cover the wishes of his children, although there were some ways in which he could add a little more revenue. He would keep his wages that were paid in cash in a big suitcase on top of the wardrobe. Although there's been many stories of Tommy being generous with his complimentary tickets from the club, all the players knew they presented an opportunity for a few extra shillings. The suitcase may have been a bit heavier than it should have been from just his Anfield salary, but few can argue with the need to bolster finances a little during this era! There would be a bonus offered if the gates were over a certain number and Tommy admitted that sometimes he would be scanning the crowd, hoping there was enough in so that his pay would be larger – often, though, he would be convinced that the stewards were pocketing some of the entry fees when the bonus didn't come. After his own ticket selling, he couldn't really complain too much!

The stardom for Tommy outside of Culcheth was certainly a lot more intense, and although he made the decision to avoid it by living away from Liverpool, he certainly knew how to entertain. Supporter Liz Hoare retold a story from a meeting with Shankly's goalkeeper:

> It was my brother-in-law who was brought up over the road from the Kop in Venmore Street, and as young kids they always used to go and play football together. They'd have a kickabout on the car park at Anfield where all the players used to come out to go to training.
>
> They used to kick a ball there waiting for the players to come out and there was a painted goal on the wall. One day, they were kicking the ball against the wall and then the players start coming out and Tommy spotted them. Without a second's thought, he ran over and went in goal for them for a few minutes. It was a small gesture but meant so much to them all.

Although this certainly wasn't the level of superstardom that many modern-day footballers have to deal with, it showed that Tommy knew how to act around supporters and that he was happy to take time out to ensure they had a happy memory to go home with. It's likely an event the Scot didn't even remember, but he made the day of the lucky few who were there and they're still telling the tale around 60 years later.

In a time before social media, this was certainly the era of a fan club, and Tommy was no different. Paul White was a young supporter of the Reds at the time and hatched his own idea as a 15-year-old to start the 'Tommy Lawrence Fan Club':

> How it started was, Ian Callaghan used to come up to our neck of the woods in Huyton as he had a relation there. I used to see him every Sunday in his car and I got talking to him, so every time they had an away game, he'd always meet me and give me the programme for it. At this same time I just realised that Tommy Lawrence was the only member of the team that didn't have a fan club. So, I asked Callaghan if he would pass on a letter to Tommy for me.
>
> The following week, Callaghan then arranged the meeting at Melwood. He took us up to the old pavilion and then it all started from there. We used to have meetings and we'd arrange football matches against other fan clubs, and the players would turn up and watch us. Tommy used to come to our house and do signings of his photographs that were going into the fan club package and then he would bring sheets they had with all the players' autographs on as well. He used to come down quite regularly to us and we

also used to go up to his. We would caddy for him and Roger Hunt, me and my friend.

People used to just send a stamped-addressed envelope to join the fan club and that's how it was done. We must have had nearly 1,000 members at the time. It was a yearly subscription, just two shillings and sixpence! We used to send paper updates about every two or three months because everything was done on typewriters then. I used to have a girl that used to do it with me and it took a fair amount of time. It didn't make any money but it was some great times.

He brought us his cup final shirt to show us one time and his medal, and when he took the cup shirt out of his bag I was really made up – all starstruck and everything! We would go up to his local, The Pack Horse, and record interviews. He'd always leave tickets at the ticket office for me to go watch the match as well, and I'd be sat with all the players' families. One time him and Roger took us home to Huyton and we were all in a Rolls-Royce. It was amazing.

It was quite the norm for players and celebrities to have fan clubs but the access that was provided to Paul White just gives a perfect illustration of how great Tommy was with the fans. A Premier League footballer meeting with a 15-year-old and providing such access to their private life is certainly not likely today. However, this was a different era and it's clear that this whole experience brought nothing but joy to all involved – including Tommy.

It wasn't just youngsters away from the game, though. In the dressing room it was clear that Tommy was a shining beacon to those making their way through the younger age groups – something he had experienced himself not too long before. Roy Evans explained this further:

> Tommy was just a very, very straightforward guy, him and Roger Hunt and they were big mates together. They were great lads and they're always trying to help even the young lads. They weren't thinking, *Hang on, these young lads might take our place*, and things like that. They were trying to make you into a better player all the time, giving you advice. They were always trying to help younger players to become better and becoming first-team players, even though it might eventually have cost them at some time. They were a great bunch of lads.

Tommy would act as a father figure to those inside Melwood, to supporters waiting for his autograph, the leader of his fan club – anyone that needed looking out for. A strong rapport with those younger than him, tied into a genuine heart that wanted to help people. This, of course, extended to his own wife and children at home.

There's another important person that hasn't yet been mentioned in detail: Tommy's wife at this time – Judy. Their daughter, Jayne, shared her story:

> Born in South Shields in 1944, her family moved to a cottage on Wigshaw Lane in Culcheth (the same Lane as my dad lived when they moved to Culcheth in 1954) when she was around six. Her dad Bill Price took over running the New Inn pub in Culcheth from his mum and dad and they lived there until she moved out when she married my dad.
>
> Mum was very creative and fashionable, she made all her own clothes and knitted too before she met my dad. I believe she was popular at school and one of her old school friends said all the boys fancied her but 'she wouldn't go out with any of us'. Mum worked as a barmaid in her dad's pub with her mum and sister Alwynne. Being creative, she also started to train as a hairdresser. She would travel to Manchester to train and became known for her 'up styles'.
>
> Mum met and started to go out with my dad when she worked behind the bar at the New Inn. He used to come in with Roger Hunt's brother Peter and a couple of their other friends. At this time, Mum

> had been given the opportunity to go and work as a hairdresser on the cruise ships but ended up giving that up to marry my dad in July 1963, something she often recalled: 'I could have had the chance to have travelled the world.'

Although dreams of grandeur cropped up, it was inevitable that the two would cross paths, but this very nearly wasn't the case. A local named Henry Page, who also ironically worked for Hunt Haulage, was out in his van one morning and saw the New Inn pub during the early hours. He saw smoke billowing out of what he thought was the chimney, but upon closer inspection it was clear that the pub was on fire. Henry ran in and saved the four inhabitants: Judy (who was a teenager at the time), her sister and their mum and dad. Henry has credible reason to claim that if it wasn't for him, Tommy's first wife wouldn't have even been alive. Pair this with the story of Billy Lawrence saving a young Tommy from drowning when he was a child, and it seems that there was some divine power bringing the pair together.

Tommy had a brief run-in with love before Judy. His failed engagement to a colleague from his office in Culcheth came to light within the family many years later but Judy was the woman on his arm for the duration of his playing days. Jayne continued with the story of one famous newspaper article:

> She had probably been more concerned that she had just finished work and hadn't been able to prepare for the shot and hoped no one would see it. Dad told me that he had turned up at training one time and the lads had cut out the article and photo and stuck it on his locker, which was the first he'd seen of it. I don't remember whether the title of the article said it, or if the lads had just dubbed it this, but my dad said it said: 'Jane Fonda comes to Culcheth.' The coat my mum is wearing in the photo is real fur, it's ocelot, and my dad had bought it for her from London, on one of his footballing trips. Not popular these days but the height of fashion in the 1960s and would have stood out in Culcheth. We often laughed at how she could have ever worn it, as it would take the three of us just to lift it!

It seemed inevitable that the most eligible bachelor and the local fashion queen would become acquaintances. This image was taken many years after their meeting and was one that Tommy would keep in his club locker. The pair had a happy relationship together. With Judy's ties to the New Inn, owned by her parents, and Tommy's local celebrity status, they were well-known and well-liked members of the village.

The pair would socialise with the Grundy family, and when it wasn't a spare few hours being spent in The Pack

Horse, Tommy would enjoy a trip to the cinema with his family and would always take Eric Jnr along with them. They would drive miles around to go to watch the latest film. Whether it be Ellesmere Port, Manchester or Rochdale, they would travel far and wide. This may seem a bit alien to film lovers today but this was the era when one cinema showed one film, so, for a bit of variety, you would have to travel a little further afield. Tommy was always very generous when everyone finally got to their destination, never afraid to put his hand in his pocket for the drinks, popcorn and whatever else his group wanted. He was a real family man and loved spending time with his children and making people happy.

As mentioned earlier, Tommy was immensely proud of his Scottish roots too and there haven't been many better periods in Liverpool history to be a Scotsman than the one in which he played. Bobby Thomson explained the connection between the countrymen in the dressing room:

> It was like a home from home because, we used to go training and then at lunch time we'd come in and have lunch at the ground together. So, we'd all sit there until we had lunch and Shankly said his speech and that was it, you know – we were inseparable. Although Tommy was a fellow Scot, he wasn't as involved. He used to head off and go home for his lunch, so it was only the reprobates left up there for lunch in the end!

It's strange to hear that Tommy was seemingly then somewhat of an outcast among the Scottish players in Melwood but it was largely down to his bond with Roger Hunt and a desire to get home to Culcheth and, probably more accurately, The Pack Horse! Living outside the city where he played his football provided the Scottish-born keeper a safe haven from the attention that would have likely plagued him within Liverpool. This did provide Tommy with a chance to offer this safe haven to others, though, and Chris Lawler talked about one trip that he and his wife made to Warrington to socialise with his team-mate:

> We went out with Tommy and his wife in Culcheth, we went to a pub, and we had a few drinks. Out of nowhere a fishmonger came around, selling fish. I never bought any, but Tommy bought some and had it all wrapped up. So, we got back in the car, and they put it in his boot and we think nothing more of it.
>
> I always remember, though, a few days later, Tommy and Roger used to alternate cars and took turns driving in together. Tommy brought Roger in this one day and I remember Roger saying, 'Fucking hell, the smell in that car!' Tommy had only left the fish in it and didn't find out until that day! I think it was in there for about a week in the end!

Although the experience of being able to socialise with his friend was probably a lot sweeter than the smell of Tommy's car, this comical interaction shows how much of a big part of the dressing room the two Culcheth residents were. The likes of Ron Yeats, Ian St John and Ian Callaghan would also be spotted visiting their mates, with Callaghan having similar stories of travelling to see his friends:

> He would invite me to his house for something to eat, and then him and Roger were golfers. I wasn't a golfer but I would walk around with them, around the golf course. They were both members of Leigh Golf Club, good old days. They were keen golfers but Bill Shankly didn't like you playing golf. If you've trained hard all week and everything else, he didn't think you should be walking around 18 holes on a golf course. The story goes that he actually rang the secretary of Leigh Golf Club to say, 'If they turn up to play golf, refuse them to go on!' They kept playing anyway because the secretary wasn't going to refuse them!

George Scott corroborated Shankly's hatred of golf, when he recalled: 'Shankly didn't like the players playing golf, he would say it makes you one-paced!' Gordon Wallace followed this up with: 'He said you're using the wrong muscles!' It certainly didn't deter Tommy from playing his golf and keeping up with the sporting lifestyle he had as a child, his love for tennis still also being present.

Shankly had not only built a great team on the pitch but a group of men who were very close off it too. Gordon Milne said, 'We weren't living in one another's pockets other than training and playing football. But, socially, everybody just got on and we used to have so much fun, so many laughs and there was no question at all about it – that created something a bit special.'

The running joke at Anfield in this time was 'the team this week is the same as last season', such was the inevitability of the same players being available for nearly every match. There was a grave fear of being injured because of the manager's behaviour towards unavailable players, which meant nobody could afford to miss a match, but the level of talent on offer meant that there was little need for rotation either. This inevitably led to a group of men being close on and off the pitch. Tommy was an easy-going part of this fun they all sincerely had together. Add to this the fact that it was also the era of Beatle-mania within Liverpool – what a time to be part of this band of brothers inside Melwood.

Rubbing shoulders with the rich and famous in Merseyside became the norm for everyone in the Liverpool squad. Bill Shankly was a big fan of the likes of Jimmy Tarbuck and Frankie Vaughan and would invite them into the dressing room to see the players before and after matches. Tarbuck explained his recollection of being part of this special era: 'I remember taking Frankie Vaughan in to meet the players for the first time. Frank said, "I can't believe we're going in here," and Bill liked the way Frank dressed. He liked well-dressed men, he loved ties and handkerchiefs. Shanks was always well dressed. Certain members of the team were my big friends. There was nothing you could criticise Tommy for in any way. He was just one of the boys.'

It seemed that Shankly also enjoyed the opportunities that came with the prestigious roles they were all in together. Although Tommy may not have been the best friends of any celebrities, he was certainly part of the scene. However, it seemed that he would prefer to be with Roger Hunt in the serenity of Culcheth and The Pack Horse. Although Roger would often frequent the local pub too, it's fair to say that he wouldn't be in there anywhere near as often as his Culcheth counterpart.

Although many of the Liverpool players felt the pair were inseparable, Tommy did have his own group of friends away from football and family. One such friend was Eric Grundy Snr, who lived round the corner from Tommy. The pair would often spend lots of time together as their children played with and looked after each other. Eric Jnr would be thrown five shillings and given the task of looking after all the younger children, while the adults went to socialise around the corner. This again was a different time when everyone's front door was left unlocked, people coming in and out, with the whole village being one family. Eric Snr explained their relationship:

> He was very jovial, a good bit of fun. We had a way of having good craic together. We used to go out drinking and we were really just a couple of drunks! He loved his gin and tonics and smoked quite a lot too. I'd given up by then but I don't know how he managed to keep going – playing football while smoking and drinking like he did. We'd be out every weekend, Saturday or Sunday, because he'd be busy at Liverpool in the week. But on a Saturday he'd be drinking his double gin and tonics and I'd pick him up from The Pack Horse at about maybe 12 o'clock, quarter past 12. He'd say he'd had a couple of drinks because he was a bag of nerves, an absolute bag of nerves – I don't think he could play unless he was half-cut. I would say he'd have three or four double gin and tonics and a packet of fags, and then he would go and play in front of 50,000 people – he was a big lad then, he could take it!
>
> He wouldn't leave The Pack Horse without three or four gin and tonics. I was saying, 'It's half past one, quarter to two, we better make tracks!' 'Okay,

we'll just finish this one!' I never saw Roger, I never saw him drinking. They never went together to the match when I knew them. I thought they would travel together but they never did. And I only really started taking him because I'd given up football myself. He loved me taking him to the club because I had a big blue Jag and he used to sit in the backseat and wave like bloody royalty!

Our wives were very friendly because the kids were all growing up together. We went on holiday a couple of years together to Fakenham in Norfolk, to the Butlin's holiday camp. We went to the local pub called The Green Man and we had some good fun. It was a very tiny village and I think everybody came out to see Tommy Lawrence! Everyone wanted his autograph, and he had time for them all. The first night we drank the pub dry! They had to go to the next pub and borrow a barrel of beer and wait for the brewery to bring more the next day! This little pub would hold about maybe 15 or 20 at the most. Every night we went in, there must have been about 50–60 who had all come round to see Tommy Lawrence. It was fabulous.

He'd get me tickets to watch him play, like when I went to Celtic Park for the 1966 European Cup Winners' Cup semi-final. I got to go up with the

> team, that was enjoyable. There was a lot of banter going on in the coach! Tommy said to me, 'Don't tell the buggers that I smoke and drink!' so I never mentioned it to any of them. Tommy was a great lad.
>
> When we were in the pub together, he was a very quiet man about his achievements – he didn't throw it about. We used to go out playing darts and dominoes and he was a likeable lad. There wasn't any airs and graces, none whatsoever. If you didn't know him, you would never think he was such a celebrity because he never acted like it at all. It was only when somebody said, 'Are you Tommy Lawrence?' I'd say, 'Oh my god,' that was it – we wouldn't be able to get away then!

It was clear that Eric and Tommy had a great friendship and one that heavily, in those days, revolved around drinking. It seems clear that the pressure of playing for a team that was challenging for league titles and in front of huge crowds was something that became too much for Shankly's stopper. Seeing as the likes of George Scott, Phil Boersma and several other of Tommy's team-mates confirmed that one of their keeper's best assets was the fact that he didn't get nervous for the big occasions, it seems this tactic worked. Conveying confidence as a goalkeeper is a huge part of your job, and whatever means Tommy used to achieve this certainly worked. It's also fair to say that it didn't really impact his performances either, although the drinking and smoking became a ritual that's far from advisable for anyone playing the game now!

Tommy asking Eric not to share any information about his extracurricular activities with his team-mates shows that he knew they were wrong. The Scot clearly didn't enjoy the fact that he grew somewhat dependant on alcohol to perform but this was not as taboo as it is in the modern era. Even up to the 1990s in English football there was a strong drinking culture, and we are talking some 30 years earlier. It wasn't the norm for all of Shankly's squad to be drinking all day, certainly not in the lead-up to a match, and it would have been a punishable offence by those within Melwood. However, it probably wouldn't have caused as much uproar as the thought of Alisson Becker sinking a few Brahmas in his local an hour before kick-off!

Having said that, though, Shankly did once famously say in an interview: 'If a man who's playing in front of the public is being well paid and he doesn't dedicate himself to the job – I would be hard on him. If I could, I'd put him in jail! Out on the road, out of society, because he's a menace.' Shankly knew his players drank but didn't like them going out clubbing or taking it too far. A Christmas party was the only time the whole squad would be out together but pockets of the team would socialise together. So, it was probably in Tommy's interest to keep this side of his life quiet. The squad would meet up in The Royal Tiger Club in Manchester Street by the Mersey Tunnel after matches and training sessions, often with the Everton squad too. This shows how accepted it was for all of them to be seen in public with a drink in hand and how relatively normal it was for drinking and football to go hand in hand at this time. What was revealed above, though, suggests that Tommy was becoming overly familiar with this drinking culture at times.

Smoking too was less of an issue than it is today. It seemed that most people were smoking in this era. Tommy and his wife, Eric Grundy and his – part of the pub culture was to be smoking at the same time. There were still adverts everywhere for tobacco products and it was in no way out of the ordinary for a footballer to have a cigarette in hand, never mind the average man in the street. Thankfully everyone, including Tommy in his later life, saw the errors of their ways, and it's certainly less present in popular culture and the sporting world today.

For the problems that Tommy was to experience in later life, this relationship with drinking definitely didn't help his post-football career. His nickname of 'The Flying Pig' certainly suggests that he wasn't at the peak of his physical condition either. But if a man can enjoy his social life and still go on to achieve the major honours he did, there's two ways of looking at him: what could he have achieved if he had treated himself as an athlete and fully committed himself to the sport? Or, what a life to be so good that you can enjoy the rewards from football, while having a full life away from the game too. Very few were teetotal athletes in this era, so the same argument can be used towards most, but whatever side you take, it's purely a personal decision. It's far from ideal to be in a position where your goalkeeper needs some 'Dutch courage' before every match, but the results were far from disastrous – yet.

Tommy lived a full and varied life away from the microscope of football in Melwood and Anfield. He managed to spin the plates and different facets of his life well, with everyone having nothing but glowing reports for how he acted. A hero to his children, an inspiration to younger players, an icon to fans and an entertainer to his friends inside and outside the game. He was certainly a man of his time, but a great man at that.

Champions, Ee-Aye-Addio & Europe

Mr T Lawrence
West Bromwich Football Club, The Hawthorns
Congratulations and good luck on your first team debut – Mr and Mrs Hunt and Peter
27 OCT. 62

TOMMY ARRIVED at The Hawthorns and was handed the above telegram as he prepared to make his long-awaited first-team debut for Liverpool. To receive such a message from the Hunt family, who had already seen their son Roger make 133 appearances for Shankly's team by the time this October afternoon rolled around, shows just how close the two Culcheth residents were. Seeing as Tommy also kept hold of the message into later life further shows how strong this beautiful bond was.

The Reds hadn't started their return to the First Division too well, and with just four victories in the first 13 matches back in the big time, it was clear that Shankly still had work to do. Jim Furnell had been signed partway through the campaign that ended in promotion from the Second Division and maintained his position in goal into the start of the new season. In the summer, the decision was made to allow Bert Slater to leave, and he was sold to Bill's brother, Bob Shankly at Dundee United, with Tommy preserving his role as second choice. However, this 13th match of Liverpool's return to top-tier football saw a performance that was less than satisfactory for anyone attached to them. Jack Rowe of the *Liverpool Daily Post* reported: 'There was no drive or thrust whatever in the Liverpool attack. They were making no headway and certainly were fortunate not to be more down.' Leicester City, a somewhat bogey team in this era, ran out 3-0 victors and Shankly knew adjustments had to come.

Three changes were made for the next match, against West Brom: Phil Ferns was in for Ronnie Moran, Gordon Wallace in for Alan A'Court and Tommy Lawrence in for Jim Furnell. Little did anyone know at the time but this was to be the final goalkeeping tinkering Shankly needed to do for the next eight years. It was initially a decision made due to Furnell's injury, as confirmed in the club's official programme: 'This game marked the League debut of Tommy Lawrence, replacing the injured Jimmy Furnell in goal, and Gordon Wallace at outside-left, and both made very creditable performances.' However, Tommy made sure to make the most of it. Given how much Shankly liked to keep his team the same if possible, for anyone stepping in to then retain their place would need a hugely impressive performance. Wallace, who was also handed his first-ever start when the Reds travelled to The Hawthorns for the match, explained his take on the day:

> We made our debuts on the same day at West Brom, 27 October 1962 to be precise. Tommy, obviously, he went from strength to strength and he had a great game that day as well. I only knew on the Friday that I was playing and it must have been the same for Tommy. The team sheet goes up on a Friday in the main dressing room at Anfield. It was the first-team dressing room for one and the reserve dressing room for the other, and you go and look at it, look for your name and then it was so good – happy days, happy days.
>
> I remember Tommy on our debut. Shanks had a quick chat with both of us. Shanks came over to me and said, because I played against Don Howe that day, 'He's on the latter stage of his career, you can run him!' It was something similar to build Tommy up and we both went out for a day we'd never forget.

Unfortunately, it wasn't the perfect maiden appearance for the young duo as West Brom ran out 1-0 victors, but both new players had shown promise. The pair were kept in for the next match against Burnley at Anfield, which meant they were both now handed a first chance to play in front of their home supporters. It was another similar tale though, where the result didn't match the performance of two of its newest players, a match where Willie Stevenson made his debut. Alf Ballard reported: 'This was for all the world like a match between the schoolboys and their masters. The youngsters (and Liverpool certainly are young these days) ran around full of pep while the masters strolled through their game, almost benevolently, knowing they could win at their leisure.'

Shankly's team was very much in transition but his belief in the talented youth players at his disposal was about to be rewarded. Tommy had made a string of impressive saves and, despite falling to a 2-1 loss, this provided enough evidence that it was worth sticking by the Scot. By the time Arsenal came to visit Anfield in November, Shankly was fielding a team with only two players (Ronnie Moran and Alan A'Court) older than 25, but it was clear that they were starting to gel. Tommy was still just 22 years old but it was reported by Derek Hodgson: 'Goalkeeper Lawrence, fast becoming an Anfield idol, went down with courage to the feet of Alan Skirton to keep the score sheet whiter than white.' It was only the youngster's fourth appearance in the 2-1 victory but it was abundantly clear that when Furnell's finger injury had subsided, there was to be no place for him in the team.

This started a run of eight straight victories and just one loss across 22 matches in all competitions. Although progress was derailed towards the end of the season, it was becoming clear that the kids were alright. An eighth-place finish in their return to the First Division meant that Shankly had seen enough to know what needed to be done for the new campaign. With the addition of one more player, the 17-year wait for success would end.

The final piece of the jigsaw was Peter Thompson, a man who quickly learned that crossing Shankly was a bad idea. During negotiations in August 1963, Thompson recalled: 'I had a friend whose father was a coach at Preston and he told me to ask for a signing-on fee. It was illegal at the time, but I knew a lot of players who'd got one.' Shankly wasn't too pleased when this idea was handed to him by a potential new player though. He said, 'I am giving you the chance to play for the greatest team, in the greatest city, in front of the greatest fans and you want illegal money!' The manager quickly turned his furious gaze to his chairman Thomas Valentine 'T. V.' Williams and barked, 'I don't want him. There's a flaw in his character!' Thompson scrambled for his potential Anfield career and insisted that it was all just a joke, and the tension within the nervy silence that followed ended with Shankly replying, 'You're a brave man asking me for extra money.' The contract was handed to Thompson, no signing-on fee was included and this flaw was fortunately ironed out.

Tommy proved that he was the man in goal too, with 45 appearances from a possible 47. A thigh injury in the second month of the campaign could have opened the door for Jim Furnell to stake his claim as Shankly's No.1 again but two matches in two days led to the swift return of Tommy. It was now clear that, whenever available, the Scot would be picked. His return to fitness was for a team in tenth place in the league and seemingly far from reaching the pinnacle of English football, but he was to be a mainstay of the success that followed.

Because of Shankly's hatred for injuries and the awareness that once you opened the door to another player, it could literally spell the end of your Anfield career, Tommy had an interesting relationship with them. His remarkable reliability saw him miss just four league matches in a six-year spell and he didn't miss an FA Cup match for eight years. It was normal to see Bob Paisley running on to tend to an injury for the often gloveless goalkeeper but it would never end in Tommy leaving the pitch. Fingers were pushed back into place, and in one match penicillin powder was put into a gash so large that Tommy Smith couldn't bear to look. In the dressing room after the match, it needed 38 stitches.

The image from this moment is as comical as it is horrific. Tommy soldiered on, though, and these cuts and scars in later life were a source of pride. His son Steve recalled:

'He would say, "That was from George Best, that one was from Denis Law, this one – Jimmy Greaves!"' They certainly don't make players like him anymore!

It's always difficult to boil an entire season of football down to a matter of moments but this winning mentality stemmed from the Second Division success into a dressing room full of young and impressive players. Shankly took all the pressure away from his men, and it was simply a message of 'go out and enjoy yourself', building each player up with every comment he made, and with Bob Paisley, Joe Fagan, Reuben Bennett and some of the more experienced players in the dressing room, it created a perfect storm.

LFCTV interviewed some of the most important players of the time and they shared their thoughts on the campaign. Ron Yeats, the captain, started by stating:

> We looked a good team and we were very, very confident in ourselves, in our own ability and we had a manager with the word 'defeat' that wasn't in his vocabulary, Shanks didn't like to talk about losing. It was winning, winning, winning and that's what happened. Every season that we played, we were always looking for the championship.

Roger Hunt, who scored a club-high 33 times in the season, added:

> We had a great run, going through to the last few games. We won three games over Easter, which got us top of the league and then we beat Arsenal 5-0 at Anfield to clinch the championship, which is great because, if you can, you want to do it in front of your own fans. It was a great performance, beating Arsenal 5-0. We had about three games to actually clinch it, so we'd have probably done it the next game if not but the atmosphere was just like a big party atmosphere. We got two goals up pretty early and the crowd relaxed and started singing, it was wonderful.

One of these experienced members of the dressing room was Ronnie Moran, who was one of the final members of the last team to play in the First Division before relegation and second-tier obscurity. He added:

> That game won us the league that year and Arsenal were a big team but we never said, 'Oh, we're playing Arsenal, we might get beat.' We just went out there and everybody said, 'Right, let's have a go.' We did that every game and we were 2-0 up by half-time and it was a good singsong for the speccys in the second half.

It was a day that also saw two penalties being saved. Ironically, one by Jim Furnell from Ian Callaghan, with the former Red managing to save some face on his return to Anfield. Tommy proved that he was still the top dog though, and his stop for George Eastham's effort (one of seven penalty saves in his career for the Reds) was crucial, as it would have made it 2-1 at the time and no doubt led to some nerves. Although Shankly's team had more games in the bank, this was the final home fixture so there was a huge desire to ensure that success was clinched in front of their own supporters.

This match is also perhaps best known for the BBC's *Panorama* show that was recorded that day and the words that John Morgan said as he stood in front of the singing and swaying Kop:

> They don't behave like any other football crowd, especially not at one end of the Anfield ground, on the Kop. The music the crowd sings is the music that Liverpool has sent echoing around the world.
>
> It used to be thought that Welsh international rugby crowds were the most musical and passionate in the world, but I've never seen anything like this Liverpool crowd. On the field here, the gay and inventive ferocity they show is quite stunning. The Duke of Wellington before the Battle of Waterloo said of his own troops, 'I don't know what they do to the enemy, but by god they frighten me.' I'm sure

> some of the players here at the match this afternoon must be feeling the same way.
>
> An anthropologist studying this Kop crowd would be introduced to as rich and mystifying a popular culture as any South Sea island. Their rhythmic swaying is an elaborate and organised ritual. The 28,000 people on the Kop itself begin singing together, they seem to know intuitively when to begin. Throughout the match they invent new words, usually within the framework of old Liverpool songs, to express adoratory, cruel or bawdy comments about the players or the police. But even then, they begin singing these new words with one immediate huge voice. They seem, mysteriously, to be in touch with one another, with 'wacker', the spirit of scouse.

This transformation of the club extended to the supporters, who were now an even more key part of what happened on the pitch. Shankly knew how to tap into their fanaticism, and the noise they provided would inspire his players, while intimidating the opposition. Roger Hunt added as the team secured their First Division title: 'I remember that day, it was a lovely sunny day and we went round the pitch after and celebrated with the crowd.' The players climbed the Main Stand to receive a homemade replica of the First Division trophy, named the Curlett Cup after its creators, brothers

Terry and Teddy Curlett. It was nothing more than an old vase painted red, with the cap from a banister lodged inside, but it was enough to recreate the trophy their team had fought so hard to clinch.

As players and fans shared their bond and celebrated triumphantly together, Shankly knew that this was just the start. Yeats added, 'As far as Bill was concerned, this is what he was building for, it wasn't any surprise for him. He had forecasted that we would win the championship and go into Europe. As far as he was concerned, this was just another season and then we forgot about it and went onto the next.'

It was an achievement for the ages and one that's perhaps lost a little because of the prestige that surrounds the name of Liverpool today. From where Shankly had brought the Reds though, this was monumental. A team stuck in the Second Division, unable to recapture their historic roots, with infrastructure crumbling around them and an aged playing staff – transformed into the best team in the country. This was a combination of many things but winning the First Division title at the second attempt was truly remarkable. Perhaps what's even more impressive, though, is that this achievement was eclipsed the following season.

* * *

It's hard to convey the importance of the FA Cup to anyone unaware of how it was viewed back then, when compared to its prestige today. Whereas now we see managers use the competition as a chance for youth and rotation players to be brought in and play some much-needed minutes, the 1960s were much different. There was no hint of rotation and the ultimate prize was lifting the trophy at Wembley.

Seeing as there was no League Cup yet and the Reds had never played in Europe before 1964, the importance of the FA Cup was clear. Add to this that the club had never won it, losing finals to Burnley in 1914 and Arsenal in 1950, then once the First Division title was secured, attention was turned to the knockout competition. The chance for Shankly to deliver this much desired piece of silverware was something he couldn't ignore and it would transform a team of league-winning heroes into legends.

After 73 years of hurt for the club, the players knew that winning the league was amazing but clinching the FA Cup would mean even more. Speaking on Liverpool FC's *Ee-aye-addio – 1965 and All That* documentary, Roger Hunt said, 'I think, if you said to anybody, "Would you prefer to win the FA Cup or the league?", they would say the FA Cup.' Not only had the Reds not achieved this before, but Everton had twice clinched the trophy in their history, so it was a constant reminder to every Liverpool fan that their achievements meant nothing until *the* cup had been won. The ridicule led to jokes that the Liver Birds on the Liver Building would fly away if the red side of the city was to ever win the trophy, and Shankly was out to right the wrongs of the past.

After a semi-final loss to Leicester City in 1963 and being knocked out by Second Division Swansea Town in the season the Reds won the league, it really felt as though it was an impossible dream. The road to Wembley in 1965 was far from easy, and when bogey team Leicester City were drawn again in the sixth round, there was almost an acceptance that another run would come to an end. Tommy recalled how the eventual replay victory at Anfield was a 'fantastic night, the noise that night – I think it was probably the biggest noise I'd ever heard that night when we beat Leicester'. It was his old friend Roger that sealed a 1-0 victory and passage into the semi-finals.

Chelsea were waiting at Villa Park and were confident that they would be cruising through to Wembley, largely down to the Reds' participation in European competition just three days earlier. Shankly used this misplaced confidence of the Londoners to his advantage though. Tommy remembered: 'Shanks never mentioned that we could be tired. He'd say, "It's about the fire in your belly boys!" and things like that, and it so happened that it worked out great for us.' Peter Thompson opened the scoring with an unlikely goal, just his fifth of the season, and even more unlikely was Willie Stevenson scoring his fourth of the campaign to make it 2-0. The unlikely hero and penalty taker took the huge responsibility and his brilliant effort booked a place in the final.

The scramble for tickets began, and Tommy recalled, 'It was amazing, there were people selling their houses for tickets, it was an amazing thing! Even for Roger and I out in Culcheth, there were people coming to our door, they were all there – fabulous!' Tommy's enjoyment at the harassment was testament to his love for Liverpool fans. Leeds United awaited, and although Willie Stevenson had a dislike for the opponents, it wasn't something his goalkeeper necessarily shared: 'Willie might have had a bad time with them, but no matter who you played against, you went in the same bar afterwards, with the same players!' Regardless of personal opinion, it was always going to be a tough meeting.

The club made the decision to take the players to London a few days early to get away from the bubbling anticipation for the match and the hordes of ticket requests that came the way of every player. Tommy explained the questionable accommodation choice: 'We were in this massive hotel and it was an old people's place, it was all ladies of leisure in their 70s and 80s. We all came out with our shorts on, took a walk around outside and when we came back, we nearly got thrown out the hotel! They were all complaining about how we were dressed and that was just before the cup final! They wanted us thrown out the hotel!'

Unhappy hotel guests aside, the preparation for the final was otherwise perfect. The players were soon met in London by the fanatic supporters, Hunt remembering: 'On the Friday night we all went to the London Palladium to see Ken Dodd and he was cracking jokes all the time about

Liverpool, which gave the lads a real boost. The next thing I really remember is the following morning when my roommate Tommy Lawrence and I were both woken up by a lot of noise by the fans outside our door.'

Finally, it came to kick-off in front of 100,000 awaiting supporters and the sea of red that met the players as they first set eyes on the hallowed turf. Queen Elizabeth was wearing red too, which was an immediate good omen for everyone of a Liverpool persuasion. 'The fans started singing for the Queen, who was there and wore red. They were singing, "The Queen's wearing red," right round the stadium!' said Tommy. This relaxed nature that stemmed from Shankly allowing people like Jimmy Tarbuck into the dressing room carried through to the fans making jokes before kick-off. The pressure that should have been present was thankfully absent.

'I think we really were confident … it was a hard game, there were really hard tackles going in. Leeds could hand them out and we could hand them out, and it probably did nullify a lot of our really good play'. Tommy was right, the match was so nullified of action that when the 90 minutes came to an end, the score remained 0-0, so for the first time since 1947 the FA Cup Final went to extra time. The Scot recalled Shankly's message to his team ahead of the extra period: 'I think he just thought we'd get it. I think he said something like: "You'll definitely get that goal, definitely," and that was the way he was.'

This confidence was again well placed, Roger Hunt finally breaking the deadlock when a mazy Stevenson run led to a brilliant cross from the heroic Gerry Byrne. Tommy's mate was at the back post to head home. The score was 1-0 to Shankly's team and victory was in sight, until …

'The ball was around about the centre circle and big Jack Charlton had come up in the box and got his head to it,' the goalkeeper remembered, watching the ball being nodded down to Billy Bremner and then sailing into the top corner of his net. As he watched the match back with six of his team-mates on the 50th anniversary of the famous meeting, Tommy jokingly said, 'I didn't move! Sorry! Willie just said that Ron Yeats was at fault and I was fine there for that goal!' The relief of hearing this 50 years later shows how much Tommy never wanted to let his team-mates down. It's fair to say there was little the keeper could have done to save the effort: 'I just looked, it was already past me and going in the top corner.'

With the match now level and no penalty shoot-outs in those days, Shankly's team had 18 minutes to decide their own fate or a replay in Manchester awaited and the prestige of lifting the cup at Wembley would be snatched from their hands. As the second half of extra time kicked off Tommy stated, 'I thought, *We can still do this*. We were still having chances.' Another chance soon came and Ian St John's head met a cross from Ian Callaghan to restore the lead. It proved to be the winner.

'When the full-time whistle went, I just went down to my knees. When I got up again, I was saying, "We've done it, we've done it!"' said Tommy. It was a dream realised for the club, for the fans and for the players too. Even the Scots knew the grandeur of the match that was broadcast around the world, and to finally achieve such a feat was unforgettable. As Ron Yeats walked up the steps at Wembley and lifted the trophy aloft, Tommy had the responsibility of holding the plinth that it had sat on. It was a role that the 24-year-old took so seriously that he barely released his grasp of it during the post-match celebrations: 'I was behind big Ronnie, he got the cup and I got the plinth and that was me for the day then! Everyone was going around with the cup and I was still carrying this bloody thing with me! Every photograph of me, I've just got hold of this base!'

Speaking with his grandson, Ryan Murray, Tommy went into further detail about what happened with him and the FA Cup plinth:

> I was sharing a hotel room with Alf [Arrowsmith], who'd come down to watch. The boys and I had been giving him a hard time as his parents would always wave him off before every game, something which made him turn bright red. So, when he came running in saying, 'Shanks is looking for you, he's not happy!' I thought it was him getting one back at

me. The next thing you know I could hear Shanks screaming, 'Where is he, Bob [Paisley]! Where's Tommy Lawrence!' I slowly went to the door and put my hand in the air. 'I'm here sir.' Shankly replied, 'Where is it?' 'Where's what, sir?' 'The bottom of the cup, where is it!' Alf was sat down on his bed beside me. He started to sink into it to hide from Shanks. I said to him, 'I've no idea, boss, I didn't even know I had it.' 'That's it, Bob! The first time we've ever bloody won the FA Cup and Tommy Lawrence has lost it!'

Shanks furiously walked away after that. I'd just won the FA Cup! It should have been the best day of my life but, after that, I spent my entire time trying to avoid Shanks. I was trying to get out of the team meal in the evening. I'd lost the bloody FA Cup plinth. I felt awful.

'Tommy, son, come over here,' Shanks shouted from across the room. 'Have you seen, son, we've found it!' 'Where was it, boss?' Shanks replied with a stern face, 'I'll tell you what, son, it was in Southend, in a coach, on the top shelf! That's about as far away as you were to Billy Bremner's volley in the final!'

This playful interaction showed both the respect that Tommy had for his manager and the control Shankly had over the dressing room. Nevertheless, his goalkeeper never really lived this down and it was a running joke for years after he had somehow managed to lose the plinth he was so determined to not let go of during the celebrations after winning at Wembley. Tommy could finally get some peace, enjoy the success and head back to Liverpool to see the supporters again.

What followed was a homecoming of epic proportions and perhaps the best indication of just how much this moment meant to the club as a whole. Hundreds of thousands lined the streets to welcome home their heroes and to thank them for an achievement none of them had ever seen before. Tommy recalled, 'We spotted before Crewe that all the houses were red and white. We looked out the window and could see all the way from Crewe to Liverpool – it was amazing!' The open-top bus drove from Liverpool Lime Street station up to the Town Hall, and the sea of supporters was further than the eye could see. 'We were looking out at the Town Hall from the balcony and you looked and you could see right down and you couldn't see anything but fans. They said there was about 350,000 there. It was absolutely amazing.'

Only once the players had witnessed the homecoming and let the emotions of a draining match soak in did they realise the magnitude of what they had just achieved. Tommy recalled what happened to his father Frank inside Wembley: 'My father was sitting beside an older man there and he'd come from Australia, and he said to him, "I'll be alright, I can die now!" He'd been in Australia for about 40/50 years then! You don't realise how serious they are really, absolutely fantastic supporters.' Frank had driven the Lythgoe family's Rolls-Royce with all the Scottish relatives on board so they could travel to London in style to watch Tommy.

This was *the* achievement for Shankly in this era. Although he'll be remembered for much more than this, winning the FA Cup was the landmark event and one he looked back at with most pride. Not winning the league again, not the relatively new competitions in Europe, but the FA Cup. Tommy recalled what Shanks told his players: 'He said, "The people will remember your names forever now in Liverpool because of that." People can just rhyme it off to you, people come and talk to me sometimes and they say, "Lawrence, Lawler, Byrne, Milne, Yeats, Stevenson …" and they can say the names of the team and these people are 60-odd, 70-odd and they can still remember the full team – it's amazing.' The team were legends immediately, and for all that came before and after it's an easy argument to make that Lawrence, Lawler, Byrne, Strong, Yeats, Stevenson, Callaghan, Hunt, St John, Smith and Thompson, as well as Gordon Milne, who missed out through injury, were a group of players whose achievements have never been surpassed by anyone else in a red shirt.

* * *

Although this success would be enough to ensure a legendary status to all who were fortunate enough to be part of it, they could have been even more revered. This FA Cup success came in the midst of a first-ever European adventure for the club and one that probably should have also ended in a European Cup victory too. Winning the league during the 1963/64 campaign meant that Shankly's team had qualified for the premier European competition, and while the FA Cup held a long-standing ambition of the club to finally get their hands on the trophy, this was a new opportunity for everyone involved.

In a time before penalty shoot-outs and away goals, matches were decided in some more unusual ways. When the European Cup quarter-final saw a 0-0 draw at the home of Cologne, a repeat at Anfield, then a 2-2 draw on neutral territory in Rotterdam, there was only one way to decide the outcome. The two league winners from their respective nations had their fortunes in the fate of a plastic disk. It was flipped into the air and, just to add more drama to the proceedings, it landed upright in the thick mud. Ryan Murray shared what his grandad remembered from the moment: '"It's only went and landed in a bloody divot," my grandad recalled. Still, with a sense of disbelief half a century later, he said, "Here we are in the quarter-finals of the European Cup and Ron and the German lad are trying to blow the coin over on to their side, you couldn't make it up!"'

Tommy and Billy Lawrence, Dailly, 1945. Courtesy of Mary Bailey

Moorston Cottage, Dailly, where Tommy was born and lived until 1949. Courtesy of Mary Bailey

Tommy's grandparents William Lawrence and Helen Lawrence. Courtesy of Mary Bailey

Johnstone grandparents and mother, 1928. Courtesy of Mary Bailey

Tommy and mother Ruby, outside family home in Culcheth. Courtesy of Mary Bailey

Liverpool youth side, 1957. Courtesy of Lawrence family collection

Liverpool squad, August 1960

Willie Carlin, Tommy and Alan Banks. Courtesy of Lawrence family collection

Tommy, August 1962

Tommy vs. Burnley, March 1963

Tommy and wife Judy, July 1963

Tommy at Leigh Golf Club, July 1963

Tommy at Anfield, August 1963

Tommy vs. West Ham, January 1964

Tommy collects his suit for LFC tour of America, April 1964

Tommy saves George Eastham's penalty vs. Arsenal, April 1964. Courtesy of Lawrence family collection

Liverpool celebrate with the Curlett Cup, April 1964. Courtesy of Michael Makison

The referee had to dig it from the earth to toss it once again. It landed red side up and, just like that, passage to the semi-finals was secured. The tale continued: 'I remember talking to Ron [Yeats] after the game and he said, "Shanks came up to me and asked what I chose. I told him I picked tails." I never forgot what Ron told me Shanks had said: "I would have picked tails myself, laddie!" Shanks just walked away with a grin on his face.'

Liverpool faced Inter Milan in the semi-finals, a two-legged tie that came immediately after the FA Cup Final. Gerry Byrne and Gordon Milne were both injured for the meeting of the Italians and they presented the crowd with the trophy that had been clinched just three days earlier. The near-55,000 inside the stadium were whipped into a frenzy, but what followed was going to be as tragic as it was magical. Ian Callaghan explained the events that unfolded when he spoke with Liverpool FC:

> The 1965 semi-final against Inter Milan was one of the greatest games I've ever played in. I listened to a tape recently of the great man Bill Shankly and he said, 'That game, it'll be hard in the history of Liverpool Football Club to beat.'
>
> Liverpool were just getting into Europe, our first European game was 1964 against Reykjavík, so it was all new, playing in Europe. Inter Milan

were then World Club champions, they'd beat a South American team and they had a fantastic team. Bringing them players to Anfield and in the semi-final of a European Cup, there was an atmosphere which was just incredible.

We'd gone to Blackpool to stay just a few days before and we arrived back at Anfield and the place was deserted, everybody was inside the stadium – it was just unbelievable. We got into the dressing room and knew it was going to be an unbelievably special night. We'd won the FA Cup on the Saturday for the first time in Liverpool's history. The great Bill Shankly, before the game, got Gordon Milne, who'd missed the FA Cup Final through injury, Gerry Byrne, who played right through the cup final and extra time with a broken collarbone, to take the FA Cup round the ground. Of course, the supporters hadn't seen it before at Anfield – so everybody went wild.

Although Inter Milan were World Club champions, they didn't frighten us. The atmosphere was just incredible when we got out on to the pitch, and we took the game by the scruff of the neck and scored in the first couple of minutes. Unfortunately, not long after that, Alessandro Mazzola equalised for Milan.

The game was 1-1 and then we got this free kick, just outside the box, which we'd practised in league

> games and, to tell you the truth, it had never ever come off. I'd run as though I was going to have a shot at goal, I'd step over the ball, Ian St John would follow behind me, he pushed the ball to Roger Hunt and he'd just push it square and I'd carry on running – which I did do and it worked! I ran on to it and put it past the goalkeeper and we scored. We tried it in many, many games afterwards and it never worked, but that one night it did work!
>
> Then, in the second half, Ian St John made it 3-1. The Kop were so quick at full time when they started singing 'go back to Italy', it was just what you'd expect from the Kop! It just shows you what that night meant to the fans, meant to the players, meant to everybody.

It couldn't have got any better at this time. You can only imagine the euphoria of supporters. Two seasons ago they were in the Second Division; now they had seen promotion, First Division winners, FA Cup winners, and now just days later seemingly booking their place in the European Cup Final at the first time of asking. If this team were already legends, then the further achievement of continental success was going to take them out of the stratosphere. That was until the second leg.

It's an important aside here to quickly mention Jimmy McInnes. The former Liverpool player had his career unfairly, but not uncommonly for his era, cut short by the Second World War. When he returned, a 32-year-old left-half was no longer needed at the club. Football in general worked to help those who entered the war in their sporting prime and returned after the fighting to a career that had ended. McInnes was afforded a benefit match to raise some funds but was also offered a job in 1948 coaching the A team. This role lasted until 1955 and his performances were so impressive that, when the untimely death of John Charles Rouse meant that a new temporary secretary position was available, the Scot was the perfect man for the job. He impressed so much again that the position was handed to him full-time.

In what was a transition from Second Division mediocrity to this victory over Inter Milan, McInnes had watched the club change beyond recognition in ten years. The growth of the club, participation in European matches, winning trophies and a larger fanbase all meant that the role was becoming more and more stressful. As reported by the *Daily Express*:

> Jimmy McInnes, secretary of Liverpool Football Club was found hanged in a turnstile booth at Anfield, the club ground last night.
>
> He was discovered by an inspector making a routine check near the Kop, the huge 'popular' stand.

> Senior detectives spent three hours at the ground last night. An inquest will be held today.
>
> While the police inquiries were going on the club directors were called from their homes for a hurried meeting in the club board room.
>
> On Sunday, when he returned triumphantly with his team to Liverpool from Wembley after winning the F.A. Cup last Saturday, Jimmy McInnes was in a jubilant mood.
>
> I travelled with 53-year-old Jimmy for part of the journey. He could talk only of the club's success. He showed no signs of strain. All yesterday he was in his office organising Liverpool's journey to Milan next Monday, in preparation for their game in the second leg against Milan on Wednesday.
>
> He spent most of his working life with the club. First as a player and then on the office side.

This commitment until the final moments of his life to ensure that his team had safe passage to Italy and everything was in place for them shows how devoted McInnes was to his job. The pressure got too much and, in an era long before mental health was so widely accepted and spoken about, the Scot suffered in silence. Although much of the success has to be afforded to Shankly and his players, there's always people behind the scenes who make the small percentage differences.

McInnes was crucial in this era of change and success, and paid the ultimate price for a role that became too big and for not living in a society that welcomed the discussion of mental health, particularly of men.

No doubt rocked by this news, the team had no option but to head to Italy eight days after the meeting at Anfield and 11 days after the FA Cup success at Wembley, to try to hold on to a 3-1 lead against the best team in the world. Bill Shankly explained what happened:

> I've never seen such hostility, smoke bombs that were purple and it was an awful feeling. And of course the decisions on the pitch … the first goal was an indirect free kick, which Mario Corso chipped into the net and they gave a goal for it. Then, Tommy Lawrence was going to bounce the ball and as he bounced it, the fella kicked it into the net. I don't think the Inter Milan players were cheats, it was the decisions. While there's a possibility that even if the decisions had gone in our favour, Inter Milan still might have beaten us … Of all the people that I've seen and met, that's the one man [José María Ortiz de Mendíbil, referee that night] he hurts me, to this day.

Ron Yeats added, 'It was proved years and years later that the referee took a bribe, he was given a villa in one of the Italian resorts. It didn't do us any good, finding this out 25 years later but they were atrocious decisions.' Among the players it was somewhat accepted that they didn't do enough on the pitch, but also that the officiating was nothing but unfair. Two goals inside the first ten minutes turned the tie on its head, and when it's discovered afterwards that the referee was bribed, the players had no chance. The final just so happened to also be played at the San Siro, Inter Milan's home stadium, and they won against Benfica. It's almost impossible to have wanted the players to have done more in this era, but when the chance of making more history, winning another trophy for the first time in the club's history, is robbed from you, it's hard not to think, what if?

* * *

To try to sum up a two-year period in a few pages seems both impossible and unfair but these were the moments that meant when Liverpool entered the 1965/66 season, they were no longer the underdog story. There were so many contributing factors to their success, so much reason to still feel hard done to and thus a fire in the belly for the players to go and achieve more.

Tommy was such a key part of this era, and to time your arrival in first-team football and your first campaign of full participation with a league title shows how perfectly aligned he was with this time and this team. It was almost meant to be and Shankly knew that his goalkeeper was a crucial part of what he wanted to go on to achieve in the coming years. The Scottish keeper seldom let him down.

A team of legends was already built, especially after what happened against Leeds United at Wembley, and now it was time to extend this legacy.

‘Sweeper Keeper’ and ‘The Flying Pig’

RONALDO IS ‘Il Fenomeno’, Lev Yashin ‘The Black Spider’, Franz Beckenbauer ‘Der Kaiser’, Ferenc Puskás ‘The Galloping Major’. Tommy Lawrence is also part of this esteemed list.

It’s not too often that a footballer is known by a nickname and not always complimentary either, but often the greatest players are handed this reward. Tommy is often coined by one of two names, either ‘Sweeper Keeper’ or ‘The Flying Pig’.

It’s often as difficult to explain the reasons for these names as it is to find their origins. Both come from quite obvious routes but their respective stories are both necessary for the story of Tommy’s life, and interesting enough to delve further into.

Sweeper Keeper

Perhaps the best way to introduce this nickname is using the words of Tommy himself:

> Bobby Graham said to me, 'The boss wants you in the office, Tommy.' So, I went and sat in this chair and he said: 'You know, the way you've been playing in the five-a-side, tackling and clearing it all the time and doing all the running for us at the back, we're going to try something this week.'
>
> So, I had to play outside my box, the 18-yard box. As soon as the game started, all I could hear was 30,000 Kopites shouting, 'Lawrence, get back in your goal!' In the end, we were losing less goals than anybody.

It was Joe Mercer who was the first to coin the phrase 'sweeper keeper' though, as the Manchester City manager couldn't believe what he had witnessed as Liverpool and Everton faced off in the 1966 Charity Shield. He said, 'He comes so far off his line, he plays like a defender.' The ability for Tommy to play as both a defender and a goalkeeper was revolutionary, an example of his talents and something that separated him from many others from this period. To not just be confined to his own penalty box but have a talent of coming out when players were through on goal and making tackles like a defender meant he was almost fulfilling the role of two players in one.

Mercer wasn't the only man outside of Anfield that marvelled at this inventiveness. John Kaye, who played against Tommy as a West Brom player, said, 'I can remember Tommy, he played like a sweeper and he didn't have to make many saves because they were so clever playing at the back. I think he could have played outside anyway as a sweeper, he was so good at reading things and he would play it straight out. He must have been the first keeper to play like that, it was unbelievable.'

It wasn't just the opposition that liked the plan. Ian St John's thoughts were: 'Tactics-wise, once we had gone into Europe and Shanks could see we were playing against different systems, we became the first team to play a flat back four ... With Tommy Lawrence coming out to the edge of the box. Our fans at the time were going, "What are you doing?"' This tactical revolution was remarkable, and for it to be so normal when considering how modern-day goalkeepers perform shows just how successful it was. This has to do with both the tinkering of Shankly and his coaching team and the talents of Lawrence that first provided them the idea and allowed them the chance to carry it out in a match.

It has been mentioned before but the presence of such elite footballing minds that were in place while Shankly was manager is nothing short of extraordinary. Bill was the boss with the bravado, oratory skills and relentless enthusiasm, while ruling with an iron fist. Bob Paisley showed with his future achievements in the most successful period in the history of the club just how influential his thoughts were.

Joe Fagan was instrumental on the training ground, noting down the sessions and maintaining a level head for anyone from the youth level up to the very top. Just in these three men alone, there would be ten league titles, four European Cups and two FA Cups during their collective tenures as manager at Anfield. This idea of playing Tommy in a new role was revolutionary but he certainly had some of the best coaches possible to help him play it.

Ron Yeats was also a big fan of this change:

> Tommy was a goalkeeper, which, if the back four had been very, very square on a through ball, you can imagine the centre-forward would be getting a lot of time but not then – Tommy would be out of his goal tackling the strikers or the wingers. He was absolutely brilliant. He'd do it in training, he loved to play out in training, I've never known a goalkeeper love to play out. He loved to be a striker, Tommy, and he could hit a ball as well.

It was hard to find anyone who was anything but supportive of seeing their normally goal-line-pinned stopper now allowed to come careering out of the box to help his defence. Chris Lawler said, 'Through the week in training Tommy would never play in goal, he'd always play out, because technically he was very good. Shankly must have seen that ability in coming out and we started pushing up a little bit more so he could clear the balls that came over our heads.'

This all came down to the passion that Tommy always held to be an outfield player, and whenever he had the chance to compete against his team-mates he would grasp it with both hands. George Scott remembered:

> At five-a-sides he would see himself as a bit of a footballer and, in the end, he became a sweeper goalkeeper. He'd come out of the goal, he was always keen to take part. He was good, he could pass around. I'm not sure he would have made the grade as an outfield player to be fair but he was good for a goalkeeper. He used to fly into tackles and he liked to slide on the ground.

Whether this was just Tommy's love for diving about in the mud following through into his opportunity to get involved in the football, or another sign of his fearlessness, it certainly seems he relished the chance to play outfield. Phil Boersma was a little more impressed with his abilities though:

> Honestly, you would think he was an outfield player when you watched him in the five-a-sides. He was as comfortable on the ball as any goalkeeper I've ever come across. I'd even say he was more comfortable on

> the ball, and at receiving back passes and whatnot, than Ray Clemence. Now Clem took goalkeeping, for me, to another level, but Tommy was very, very comfortable because he had to be, because Shanks wanted to see us push up.

As nicknames go, this one is testament to the talents of Tommy and Liverpool in this era. It personifies the way in which the 'Liverpool way' and the boot room boys were so far ahead of the rest of the country. This method is used by nearly every team in the world today, and if Tommy Lawrence and Liverpool are attributed credit for being the first to do this, then it shows that they were trailblazers. This one tactical tweak and the ability of a goalkeeper who was hungry for any opportunity to play off his line illustrates why the Reds went on to dominate for the next three decades.

The Flying Pig

Comical yet potentially offensive, the name is rather self-explanatory but hinted at Tommy's physique being a little larger than that of his team-mates, yet his reflexes and flexibility were far superior. Although Joe Mercer is widely attributed credit for 'Sweeper Keeper', it's not actually known who was the first to decide that 'The Flying Pig' was the right way to describe the acrobatic Scot, but it certainly stuck.

It seems that there are several opinions in place on who came up with it. Bobby Thomson shared his thoughts: 'It was started by the players, St John and that, all the players. I don't know if he liked being called it, but he got it!' Kevin Lewis added: 'I think it was started by the players. I didn't want to be the only one to say it but, for someone so big, he could get across the goal – he was a big chap.'

Others, including Chris Lawler, were sure that it was the supporters: 'I think the Kop gave him the name. The players would never do that. He never seemed upset by it, I think. It's just the scouse humour isn't it?' George Scott agreed: 'It was a fan thing but I'm sure Tommy knew exactly that it was a compliment. They thought he was a legend, because he was.' Ian Callaghan was of this thought too: 'No, no, not at all. It was more of a fan thing than the players. Even today when people mention him, they say, "Oh, The Flying Pig!" So, he's got quite a strong legacy from that.'

The confusion around the name is quite clear, but in the words of Phil Boersma:

> We all knew Tommy was overweight and, obviously, I don't think it was any of the lads who gave him that nickname, 'The Flying Pig'. And so, I don't really know where that comes from, but if Chris Lawler said it was the fans, that is probably right, because he would have been there right from the beginning.

> Tommy was obviously overweight. But, hey, it didn't stop him from doing what he did, and that was save shots!

Regardless of who came up with it, though, it seems the assertion that the goalkeeper was carrying a little too much weight was widely agreed upon. Ron Yeats boldly claimed, 'We used to call him "The Flying Pig". He was a little bit overweight, Tommy, but he was a good goalkeeper.' George Scott recalled the methods Tommy used to try to maintain his weight:

> How can I put it? Physique-wise, he probably did look a little bit overweight if anything. He used to wear them plastic things at the start of pre-season. Tommy Smith and Tommy Lawrence, they used to wear these, they were wrapped up in plastic, trying to sweat more and get the weight off. It was all the big lads, Ronnie too. They needed to get the weight off for the season because Shanks would have a go if you weighed too much.

Although goalkeepers are often treated a little differently anyway, there's no chance that Shankly would have allowed Tommy to be hugely overweight. His and the other players' efforts to lose a few extra pounds shows that it wasn't abnormal for any of them to return after a summer a little larger. Seeing as the nickname was only afforded to the man in goal though, perhaps we can be kind and say red must have been more slimming than green!

Tommy wasn't the only one who had trouble controlling his weight and he was far from the worst trainer too. Willie Stevenson recalled: 'Tommy was a good trainer. I wasn't, I was always at the back! I was always last, sometimes I got back from training and in the dressing room when they were going home! It would take me that long. Tommy, me and a few others used to try and hide when we were doing laps but they soon cottoned on to it!'

Tommy certainly seemed to struggle with his weight and, at times, it was visible on the pitch, but none of his team-mates seemed to think it was something that was of any concern, or a risk to his performance. One thing that's certain, too, is that Shankly would have nipped it in the bud if he thought it was affecting on-field playing ability.

If we try to ignore the potentially offensive undertones of the name, though, it all boils down to a compliment for the way in which Tommy could fly through the air. His friend from Culcheth, Eric Grundy Snr, said:

> I'll tell you one thing about Tommy, he was the first goalkeeper I actually saw fly. He was touching balls out of the top corner. That was unseen before but

> he perfected that and that's why he was known as 'The Flying Pig' in the end. Oh god, I tell you he was a flyer. Long before the other ones came along and started to imitate him and start trying to get the top ones in the corner. He was really good and they certainly taught him how to fly!

Not just an acrobatic marvel, though, this flying could also be attributed to the fearless nature in which Tommy would dive at people's feet. He often showed little concern for his own welfare and that's why Gordon Wallace thought he was given the name: 'I would say he was brave, a great stopper and fearless and I think the flying pig describes that.'

Probably the best way to summarise 'The Flying Pig' is how the man himself would have felt when he was called it. Tracey shared her memories of her dad's history with the name:

> What my dad said is, when he came back from a pre-season tour of America, when they used to get six weeks off, he came back quite big! I think when they went to America, something must have been said then. But my dad loved it though! Whether it was players or fans, it wasn't clear, but it started in 1964. My dad didn't have an issue with it, his shirt was always a bit tight and he wasn't big, big.

Tommy's son Stephen added: 'He was only 13 stone when he was playing – I'd love to be 13 stone!'

Perhaps the mystique of the name had added some mental pounds to supporters' minds, but to hear that Tommy never took it as anything but a sign of love from the fans means that it's a good thing it's such a big part of his legacy. If it's not 'oh, the bloke who got interviewed by the BBC', the first thing to come out of most people's mouths when they hear the name Tommy Lawrence is 'The Flying Pig'. His name almost defines his career, and even if you haven't seen him play, it presents a rather vivid image. Yes, a man who may have struggled a little with his weight but also a goalkeeper who could fly through the air unlike many who came before and after him.

* * *

It seems 'The Flying Pig' is both a little less complimentary but also perhaps better associated with Tommy today. To be known as the first 'sweeper keeper' would probably be a nicer and grander title for him to hold, but to have a choice of two just shows his impact on the game. The ability of Liverpool at the time is personified by being called a sweeper, and the thought of a pig in goal may take away from what Tommy achieved.

In reality, though, there's no reason to have to pick one. You can call him whatever you like, reference the interview, coming off his line, diving through the air or anything else, but it's hard to know Tommy for any reason other than being a great footballer and a fantastic man. They say you die twice: once when you pass away and again when nobody remembers you. With a name like 'The Flying Pig' and a book title thirsty to cover all bases and mention his other nickname, alongside his actual name too, it's hard to think anyone will ever be able to forget what Tommy Lawrence did. These two nicknames show his importance and ensure that he's likely never to be forgotten.

'The Best Goalkeeper in the Land'

AS WE return to the chronological action of Tommy's life, he was playing for a Liverpool team that had just won the FA Cup, and the season before had clinched the First Division title. This meant that when the 1965/66 season began, Shankly's team were among the favourites to go on and clinch yet more silverware.

This was uncharted waters for everyone associated with the club, as it had been 18 years since the last major trophy, so an entire generation of Liverpool supporters didn't know what it meant to be successful. It wasn't just the fans either. This team was a blend of fresh talent and a few older heads, none having experienced success before. It was a new feeling of superiority, and having a target on their backs, something the FA Cup holders soon discovered.

The Reds were at home against Chelsea, a strong opponent to face in the third round of the FA Cup, and a team that would end the season fifth in the league. With this being the first FA Cup tie since the heroics against Leeds at

Wembley, expectation was high for Shankly's men and it was an action-packed start to the match. Peter Thompson darted down the left wing and his deep cross found the head of Roger Hunt, who nodded it down to Ian St John to fire home in just the second minute. The Londoners were as quick off the mark, though, and an 18-year-old Peter Osgood made an immediate impact with an equaliser inside the first ten minutes. Such was the performance of the goalscorer that it led to Kenneth Wolstenholme to state on *Match of the Day*: 'What a mover this boy is! What a beautiful run! I'm giving away my age but that reminded me of David Jack at his best!' The youngster was impressive on a fine display by the team from Stamford Bridge, and not long after the start of the second half their tally was doubled, with Bobby Tambling's goal enough to dump Shankly's team out of the cup at the first hurdle.

This was to be a crucial match in the context of the season. As Tommy Docherty's team marched on, the Reds were left to dust themselves down. Eric Todd wrote in *The Guardian*: '[Liverpool] surely must suspect, like the Kop, that they are not quite as indestructible or as infallible as they thought they were. Or as they have been led to believe they were.' For the first time in a while, there was doubt about the rigour of the Reds.

This meant a refocus on the league, the 'bread and butter' for all supporters, and an opportunity for the Reds to reassert their dominance. The season had started well, the Reds brushing aside 'bogey team' Leicester City in a 3-1 victory away from home, but the first match at Anfield brought everyone back down to earth. The 1-0 loss to last season's 18th-placed Sheffield United was crushing but proved to be one of only two home defeats the Reds would experience all season.

The next few weeks saw five goals fired past West Ham, then when neighbours Everton crossed the park to Anfield, another five were scored again. It was a day to remember for everyone present, and Horace Yates described proceedings in the *Liverpool Echo*:

> 'Ee Aye Addio, we're all going home,' chanted one of the most deliriously happy crowds which have ever assembled on the slopes of Anfield's Spion Kop. There were ten minutes left; Liverpool were four up. I guarantee not one of them could have been dragged from his position. Their gibe was merely a turning of the knife in the already mortal wound with which Everton were afflicted.
>
> The fact that this was probably the most one-sided 'derby' clash ever seen in the series of ninety-three, mattered not at all to Liverpool's following. Every kick, thrust and threat brought them new joy, but what of the Everton throng? This was humiliation, utter and complete, a side not only overwhelmingly

> beaten, but with their spirit shattered. Candidly I never believed the modern Everton could be subjected to such indignities.

A 3-0 loss to West Brom in late October was a match of note in this early season merry-go-round of results. It was the second time Shankly's team had lost in four outings, also a match where Tommy Smith had to present the referee with a hard-boiled egg that had been thrown towards him from The Hawthorns' crowd, leading to a public announcement for no further fan misbehaviour or the match would be called off. Although, according to Jack Rowe in the *Liverpool Daily Post*, 'Lawrence did nothing really wrong, but for the rest it was a miserable day.' The Reds sat in eighth, but a reaction was coming.

This was the lowest position Shankly's team would hold for the rest of the season, winning 4-0 in the next match against Nottingham Forest at Anfield, which saw them leap into fifth. A 2-0 victory at Hillsborough, where it was reported that 'Lawrence's greatest achievements were in stifling attacks by anticipation and safe handling while they were still manageable', saw the Reds climb to second. The successive five-goal drubbings over Northampton Town and Blackburn Rovers in November meant that the Kop choir could sing 'Ee-Ay-Addio, we're top of the league' for the first time since clinching the title in 1964.

Only once the scoreline reached 4-1 against Blackburn with under ten minutes remaining did the cautious supporters allow themselves to sing about a table-topping performance. This guarded support was growing in confidence as each week passed and the ever-widening gap to the likes of Burnley, Leeds United and West Brom grew bigger. By the time Liverpool travelled to Chelsea in December for the first league meeting between the pair, the Reds were still top and were firm favourites to both win the match and go on to clinch the title again. Horace Yates reported:

> [George] Graham, an extremely dangerous marksman with foot and head, shot through a crowd, with Lawrence clearly unsighted. The way in which the goalkeeper saw the ball and grabbed it at the second attempt as he dived on the line was for me the game's highlight.
>
> The advance of Lawrence to a position to-day where he is among the most accomplished goalkeepers in football has been one of the outstanding events of an outstanding Liverpool season. In the first half, with courage most rare, he flung himself at the ball in front of goal, realising full well that [John] Boyle was following through at the ball, come what may.
>
> Lawrence collected the ball and received a kick high on his cheekbone, only an inch or so from his eye.

> The goalkeeper's daring and reliability never faltered. If he was ever good enough to play for Scotland, his claims to-day must be considerably greater. Here another spectacular Anfield story of triumph.

It was a match decided by a Roger Hunt goal with a little over 15 minutes remaining, but the efforts of the ever-most improved goalkeeper couldn't be ignored. Kenneth Wolstenholme said on *Match of the Day*: 'It's going to take a very fine side to stop this Liverpool march, the way they're playing at the moment. They're a strong side, they haven't got a weakness from goal to outside-left.'

The excitement around Shankly's team and football within England was at an all-time high. Chelsea, Leeds United, Manchester United and Liverpool were all to reach European semi-finals this season, the World Cup was about to be hosted in England, but Merseyside was *the* place to be. Wirral-educated and former MP for Huyton Harold Wilson was prime minister, The Beatles had just clinched their ninth of 18 number-one singles, Everton were about to win the FA Cup and the Reds were still firmly top of the league.

The table-toppers travelled to Burnley in April knowing that a point would clinch the title but things didn't go to plan. The mud bath at Turf Moor hampered the passing game that Liverpool were so widely praised for. Willie Irvine's goal inside ten minutes bloodied the noses of the Reds and they never recovered. When Ralph Coates's left-footed effort was curled past Tommy in goal it was clear there would be no champagne corks flying just yet. The Lancashire club were second in the league but still seven points behind Liverpool, so although it was no doubt a brilliant performance from the home team, the question was still when and not if the league title would be brought back to Merseyside.

Winning the league is always a luxury but if anyone wants to be totally honest, the chance to win it in front of your own fans is preferable. Although defeat at Burnley delayed the party, it just helped make it even sweeter. It was again Chelsea that were the opponents for a crucial match, and such was the level of respect and expectancy that the Reds would go on to win the league that Tommy Docherty asked his players to perform a guard of honour as the Liverpool team ran on to the pitch, while the band played 'Oh When the Saints Go Marching In'.

The Kop were in fine voice on a sunny afternoon at the end of April, despite a goalless first 45 minutes. Within three minutes of the restart, though, Roger Hunt's cross-come-shot was kindly deflected into his own net by opposition keeper John Dunn to hand the soon-to-be champions the lead. It eased the tension within the stadium and loosened the shackles that title-deciding nerves seemed to hold over the home team. The rigidity of a stern Reds defence meant that a 1-0 lead had been as good as a win in many matches this season but that didn't stop the Reds from wanting more.

Bert Murray dealt a sucker-punch, though, as totally against the run of play he found himself beating Ron Yeats to the ball and poking it past Tommy Lawrence to make it 1-1. Although only a point was needed, the nerves were once again palpable inside Anfield. After losing to Burnley and now drawing with Chelsea, thoughts of an improbable collapse began to creep into everyone's minds. Cometh the hour, cometh the Culcheth hero again. Roger Hunt's dancing feet inside the Kop end penalty box freed up some space, and his effort was too much for Dunn to handle again. Speaking humbly about the moment, the goalscorer said, 'I think it was fortunate. I'd say it was a goalkeeping error but they all count!' It created a party atmosphere once again inside Anfield and the supporters began a chorus of 'Oh When The Reds Go Marching In!' The full-time whistle finally confirmed the league winners. After being top since November it was never in doubt that this day would come, but a third trophy in three seasons had been confirmed at the final home match of the campaign.

The Football League was as prepared as it had been two years earlier and once again the services of the Curlett Cup were required. As the players accepted the makeshift league trophy, Bill Shankly came on to the pitch to a huge roar and it was clear who was the best team, the best manager and the best fans in England, in a year that will forever be remembered for an England World Cup win too. Just 15 players had been used in all competitions, 14 in the league, 12 of whom had played 22 times or more, nine having missed two or fewer matches in the league campaign. Tommy played every single match in all competitions. Shankly's team were at their relentless pomp and he had such reliance and trust in such a small group of players that he seldom wanted to rotate.

Speaking after the match, the manager performed a joint interview with the Chelsea boss and claimed, 'It's a big thing to win the championship. I think the fact that you beat us here in the cup was responsible for us winning the league.' Shankly still hadn't forgotten the pain of being knocked out of the FA Cup and had clearly used it as inspiration for his players to ensure they still made something out of the season.

After showing his class before the game, Tommy Docherty did so once again afterwards, when he replied, 'Yeah it's true, you did well – you've got a great side, Bill. You deserve it, mate, it couldn't have gone to a better bloke.'

Shankly responded with, 'We're happy about it, Tommy, it's amazing, even after that game today, we could have lost today and we still would have won the championship!'

The superiority of Liverpool was clear to see and plenty of this stemmed from a fierce defence. Chairman Sidney Reakes was so proud of his team, his defence and mainly his goalkeeper:

> I remember well, the experience of Tommy Lawrence last season, when sometimes he did not appear to be the perfect answer to Liverpool's prayer. 'Give him a chance,' said Bill. 'He is young; he is still learning. Nobody can yet say how good he might become.' Lawrence has repaid that consideration by becoming the most improved goalkeeper in football.
>
> In nineteen league games he has not conceded a goal. He would be the last to claim all the credit for that, for the defence in front of him has been almost frightening in its efficiency. Yet, his part is beyond question.
>
> Otherwise you would not find Mr Shankly quipping: 'I am thinking of giving Tommy special training all through the summer. He has had nothing to do all winter!'
>
> Everybody knows how sound Lawrence has been and one of his most satisfying moments must have been to hear the Kop acclaim him as 'the best goalkeeper in the land'.

This was the peak of Tommy's career and the peak of Shankly's first great team at Anfield. Little did anyone know at the time, but after a five-year run of being Second Division champions, FA Cup semi-finalists, First Division champions, FA Cup winners and European Cup semi-finalists, to winning the league again in 1965/66, the glory days wouldn't last. Few would have anticipated that Liverpool would then go 2,451 days, or nearly seven years, without clinching silverware again, and that there would be a different man in goal when this happened.

There's time to go into all of this later, but at this point Tommy was handed the Curlett Cup and celebrated in front of the Liverpool supporters on what was to be his final great day as a Red. His story in football and in life is far from over but it may well have peaked on an April afternoon in 1966.

* * *

It was another first for the club in Europe too and, although there was no place for Liverpool in the European Cup this year, it was time for a maiden appearance in the European Cup Winners' Cup. The competition had four two-legged ties against other cup winners from Europe, ahead of a final at Hampden Park at the end of the season. Shankly was out for revenge for the events against Inter Milan in their last European campaign.

What makes the feat of being top of the league for 25 of the 42 matches of 1965/66 special is that it was all done in the context of another uncharted European charge. Although the European Cup was the premier tournament on the continent, this was another opportunity for Shankly's team to make history at Anfield. Ties against Juventus, Standard Liège, Honvéd, Celtic and Borussia Dortmund shows the standard of opposition in the competition, though, and it was far from straightforward to plot a route to the final in Glasgow.

Facing Juventus away in the first round meant a return to Italy, four months after the controversial visit to Inter Milan. Shankly gave his team clear instructions to defend and bring back any result they could to Anfield two weeks later. Albert Barham wrote in *The Guardian*: 'Even though it was so much a lesson – and a negative one at that – of tactical defence. Juventus are past masters at this style which is doing so much to destroy football as a spectacle. They even played defensively in front of their own supporters and so far this season in five matches have now scored only twice, and it need hardly be said concede none at all.'

This negative and defensive match meant it was far from a classic, but leaving Italy with a 1-0 loss, after a speculative long-ranged effort from Gianfranco Leoncini flew past Tommy, was accepted as a positive result. This European experience taught the team to not chase an equaliser but instead to wait for the Anfield meeting. Whistles and renditions of 'go back to Italy!' met the visitors, who would soon be leaving with a 2-0 defeat in their luggage and a swift exit from the competition.

This experience helped right some wrongs of the previous year, and the Reds the steamroll Standard Liège with home and away victories to set up a glamour tie with Honvéd. Shankly again set out to defend in the first leg, away in Budapest, and then attack at home – it worked. A 0-0 draw was followed by a 2-0 Anfield victory, with Chris Lawler scoring his fourth goal in six European matches that season. It set up a meeting of minds as Bill Shankly pitted his wits against Jock Stein's Celtic in the semi-final, away once again in the first leg.

The message was clear, another Italian job where the Reds would do anything to kill the atmosphere and get back to Anfield with a chance of winning the tie. Gair Henderson wrote in the *Evening Times*: 'They may call it football down on Merseyside … it may have taken Liverpool to certain victory in the English League Championship … but spare me, please, from another dose of the boredom served up by Liverpool at Celtic Park.'

This pragmatic approach didn't stop the Scots winning 1-0 but did make them think that the return at Anfield would be a walk in the park, due to the lack of any attacking flair on show from the Reds in Scotland. However, a Tommy Smith free kick and a Geoff Strong header on the Anfield mud bath ensured another special European night under the lights. Shankly's master European plan had worked a dream. Bear in mind that this was the Celtic team that the following season would be called the 'Lisbon Lions', as they became the first British club to win the European Cup.

Far from Liverpool's exciting league form, these away stalemates in Europe paved the way for second-leg comebacks and laid a blueprint for many years of defending away and attacking at home. Another trip to Scotland was on the cards, and five days after winning the league against Chelsea at Anfield the Reds were to face Borussia Dortmund in the European Cup Winners' Cup at Hampden Park in Glasgow.

Tommy was one of four Scots who made the journey back home for the massive match. It was the same quartet that had started in the victory over Leeds United in the FA Cup Final the previous year. Ironically, their numbers (1 – Lawrence, 9 – St John, 6 – Stevenson, 5 – Yeats) made up the numbers of the year of their famous Wembley achievements. Tommy had brought Eric Grundy Snr along for the coach journey from Liverpool to Glasgow, and many more members of the family made the trip to support him in his first European final. Willie Stevenson had tickets for his brother and dad, and it was a match that meant a lot to everyone, especially the healthy Scottish contingent. Ian Callaghan said, 'It was a massive game for the Scottish lads, playing at home. It was a massive game.'

With the final being a one-legged face-off between the two teams, there was no place for the defensive tactics Shankly had deployed earlier in the tournament. The Liverpool fans let out a loud rendition of their new anthem, 'You'll Never Walk Alone'. All eyes were on how the Reds would fare in the hunt for an unprecedented double, and to become the first British club to claim a European trophy. The Germans had three players within their line-up (Hans Tilkowski, Lothar Emmerich and Siegfried Held) who would start in the World Cup Final for West Germany at Wembley that summer, with just one Liverpool representative (Roger Hunt) playing in that famous match.

Often Shankly would pass the instructions to his players of 'make sure the first touch is an easy one', which encouraged a passing game. However, a reminder to them all to be strong and to Tommy to ensure the ball was in the opposition half by clearing his lines shows that the commands to the goalkeeper were a little different. The Reds went out on the front foot and seemed determined to make an immediate impact. It wasn't going to be an easy feat to beat the German defence though, and the pools of water that sat around the outside of the pitch illustrated the dreary conditions that met the final. A near-waterlogged playing surface, a not fully fit Roger Hunt and a tough opponent meant that success was always going to be difficult.

The near-42,000 supporters inside the stadium were soaked through as the half-time whistle signalled the end of a scoreless first 45 minutes. The start of the second half saw a positive show of Liverpool's willingness to open the scoring, and by the hour mark Dortmund had barely laid a glove on them. That was until Gordon Milne's misplaced pass was quickly intercepted by Rudi Assauer, who found the dangerous Siegfried Held. After a quick one-two with Lothar

Emmerich, he was allowed space for a strike at goal. He hit a thunderous volley from the edge of the box, which rifled past Lawrence to put the Germans ahead, which meant the Reds had to start attacking again, and quickly.

They didn't have to wait long, less than ten minutes, in fact, when Peter Thompson went on another mazy run. After weaving past three men, appeals from Dortmund followed as they believed the ball had run out of play for a goal kick. The linesman waved his flag and many defenders stopped. The referee, however, didn't believe it had left the pitch, so allowed the cross to find the feet of Roger Hunt, who found the top corner to level the scores. Mass appeals from the Germans followed, as hundreds of Liverpool supporters stormed on to the pitch in celebration. Replays were far from conclusive so it looked a fair decision from the French referee. Game on.

Try as they might, Liverpool couldn't find a winner. Roger Hunt had a huge chance in the final seconds but his injured ankle on a heavy pitch meant it simply passed him by. The full-time whistle went and Shankly came on to the pitch with Reuben Bennett to pass on some final instructions ahead of extra time. Liverpool were in charge and the fitness instilled in the players from their expert coaches surely meant it was a matter of minutes until they found the lead for the first time.

The second period of extra time had not long begun when Tommy Smith overstretched for a tackle and a free kick was awarded to Dortmund. Alfred Schmidt played a long ball to Siegfried Held but Tommy showcased his sweeper keeper abilities as he flew out of his goal and managed to snuff out the chance. However, this expert piece of bravery only led to the ball rolling out towards the right wing and a quick-thinking fan favourite Reinhard Libuda lofted a speculative effort towards the unguarded goal. It looped over Lawrence and Ron Yeats, with the defender desperately leaping to defend his goal. However, the shot, which looked goalbound, instead rebounded off the post and hit the falling Yeats on the line. It was a show of skill from the winger but also a huge piece of fortune as he managed to force an own goal of disastrous proportions. It was against the run of play, with the Germans timing both of their goals to perfection in order to sucker-punch the Reds.

The Liverpool fans restarted a sombre rendition of 'You'll Never Walk Alone' as the final seconds ticked past. It was an unfamiliar feeling of defeat and dejection, and although the Reds had given a good account of themselves, two mistakes had been capitalised upon and the final ended in heartache. Shankly bemoaned the 'silly goals' that were conceded, which went against his usual positive mantra and told the story of an opportunity missed to make more history.

The club celebrated the success of the last four seasons at the end of this campaign, as if they too recognised that this was a remarkable level of achievement yet also possibly the peak. Sidney Reakes outlined the club's ambition to be the first English winners of the European Cup: 'A mighty order? Of course, but then Liverpool are a mighty team. We are proud of them.' Each player was asked to name their most vivid memory of the last four years, and Tommy said, 'Saving the penalty in the Arsenal game when we won our first championship. George Eastham took it.' His crowning moment was the first title they won together as a team and the save that maintained their lead in a crucial match.

Liverpool were at their peak but hadn't managed to clinch the European success they deserved. No doubt a tremendous team in the league and their special cup tactics had made them a force to be reckoned with. What was quietly happening, though, was too many miles being clocked up by such a small group of players. Tommy played 390 times in all for Liverpool, but 272 of them came in a five-season window. Although goalkeepers have less impact on their bodies than those playing outfield, the repeated success and progression in the league, FA Cup and in Europe meant they were being overused. Roger Hunt is a good example, as he was declared fit for the final but clearly wasn't. This fear of being injured and the lack of rotation had started to take its toll. While competing for the biggest trophies makes it hard to argue there's a need to keep changing a successful team, it was probably time in 1966 to start tweaking a line-up that would remain nearly unchanged until 1970.

Tommy too was at his peak, and to be labelled 'the best goalkeeper in the land' at this time shows how far the whole team had come together. Making a team of winners is no easy feat but creating another one in their image is almost twice as hard, and this was telling in the years that were to come.

Scotland

DESPITE LEAVING Scotland at such a young age, there was never any doubt about how committed Tommy was to his nation and how proud he was to be Scottish. To win Liverpool's first European trophy at the home of Scottish football may well have been a feat that would have been hard to beat by any others in his illustrious career but it wasn't to be. In fact, this feeling of nearly achieving an ultimate ambition in Hampden Park is probably the perfect illustration of his international football career.

If Liverpool were the team of this era and Tommy Lawrence was declared, even if it came from the chairman of his own club, the best in the land, then why did he only manage to receive three caps for his nation? The answer is probably Bill Brown. The former Tottenham goalkeeper also had his fair share of success in the 1960s, winning the First Division, FA Cup (twice) and European Cup Winners' Cup, doing all of this by 1963. This rise to prominence in the years right before Shankly catapulted the Reds out of the Second

Division and into the limelight meant that when Scotland manager Ian McColl picked his goalkeeper between 1960 and 1965, Tommy never stood a chance. This loyalty to Brown made it hard for anyone to force their way into the team, especially the man who guarded the net at Anfield every week.

Jock Stein, John Prentice, Malky MacDonald and Bobby Brown were all handed the chance to manage the national team in the years after 1965, which also coincided with Tommy's top-level career. This managerial merry-go-round meant there were plenty of different keepers handed an opportunity between the sticks. In the ten-year period between 1960 and 1970, 14 different keepers wore the No.1 jersey for the Tartan Army but only Bill Brown made it to double figures in terms of appearances.

Ian McColl handed Tommy his debut for Scotland in 1963 but he didn't return to the squad until 1969, under Bobby Brown. This meant that three successive Scottish bosses didn't select Tommy at all. This lack of belief in his talents certainly hampered his ability to make an impact on the national team. Given that his international career spanned only three matches, it's probably best to assess them individually.

09/06/1963 – Republic of Ireland vs Scotland

Ian McColl was often spotted watching Liverpool play, but with the likes of Ian St John (21 caps), Ron Yeats (two caps) and Willie Stevenson (0 caps) playing for the same team, it was never clear whether his eyes were on Tommy or the rest of the Scottish lads. An FA Cup semi-final defeat to Leicester City in April was penned as the reason St John missed out on the next set of Scottish fixtures, but by the end of the season he and Tommy managed to catch the eye of the Scottish squad selectors. The *Liverpool Daily Post* reported in May:

> What a wonderful day it was for Liverpool F.C. yesterday when five of their players were named to take part in international tours abroad at the close of the season – Melia, Milne and Hunt, all chosen by England, and St. John and Lawrence for Scotland … The sensational rise to fame this season by Tommy Lawrence means that Liverpool can now boast an international representative in every department of their side.

Despite this great day for Liverpool and for Tommy, it came in the context of one key decision. The same report also stated: 'Scotland's first choice goalkeeper, Bill Brown of Tottenham, had previously indicated that he wouldn't be available because of a club tour to South Africa.' No doubt a huge achievement for the stopper living in Culcheth but only possible due to a withdrawal by the man he had failed to displace. It wasn't the first international moment for Tommy though, with two

Under-23 international appearances already under his belt. First selected in December 1962, the local press in Culcheth were delighted to share the news:

> A record that will never be broken, say folk of Culcheth, who have two international footballers living in the village, both playing for the same team and both selected to play in Under-23 international sides. Latest villager to be capped is Tommy Lawrence, picked for the Scottish Under-23s against Wales at Aberdeen. Two years ago the residents were drinking toasts to Roger Hunt, another Liverpool player who was capped for England Under-23s.

Such was the pride of Tommy that in his private collection of telegrams he kept from highlights of his career, the most relating to one match was this Under-23 debut. Family and friends were so proud of his achievement in heading to Pittodrie in Aberdeen to represent his country at youth level that you can only imagine the feeling they had watching him perform for the senior team. What's also clear is that Tommy loved it too. His sister Mary shared details about the family's pride in being Scottish, which was something that was held above all else in his footballing career. Had it not been for the fact that his performances at Anfield, which certainly warranted more than three international caps, were so much better rewarded than his achievements with the Tartan Army, he may well have viewed memories of representing his nation above those of playing for the Reds.

Back to his debut, though, where it was a day for fringe players to be handed a chance to impress in a summer friendly away to the Irish. Tommy was joined by Leicester City's Frank McLintock as the only debutants on the day, but, as reported by John Rafferty for *The Scotsman*, they had differing levels of success:

> It should be said right away that only five of the eleven that lined up played in the team who beat England at Wembley, but this latest defeat shows how thin is the crust of great Scotland players. Only [Billy] McNeill of the new men came through as a player of class.
>
> Lawrence was a badly balanced goalkeeper who dropped the ball almost disastrously in the first few seconds and thereafter spread uncertainty throughout the defence.

It took just six minutes for Ireland's captain Noel Cantwell to beat Lawrence in goal and the unease in the new man's performance was seemingly contagious. The match report continued: 'Lawrence came out and missed the ball and six shots were deflected desperately before the situation was cleared and that was how near Scotland came to an even worse defeat.'

This was the second of a three-match tour and the only one Tommy featured in, as well as being his last for six years. The form of Tottenham's Bill Brown (who beat a South African National League XI 5-2 the same day), a broad group of Scottish goalkeepers and his own inability to impress on the international stage meant it was simply a day that passed Tommy by. At this point, the true success of Lawrence as a Liverpool player had yet to arrive. So, he had to show great strength of character to dust himself down and reset his focus on what was to be a trophy-laden period on the horizon.

Scotland selectors were uninterested in his performances, though, and, despite often being part of squads, the long wait for a return to on-field first-team action began.

16/04/1969 – Scotland vs West Germany

It would have been fair for Tommy to think that his one and only chance of a Scotland cap had been and gone. Yet, with each managerial change that occurred for the Tartan Army, there was always a lingering hope that his performances for Liverpool could lead to a triumphant return. Either that or more injuries to peers could provide him with another chance, although Tommy would never be a man to think like that. Ian McColl handed a debut to the stopper but never picked him to start again after the match against Ireland. Jock Stein, John Prentice and Malky MacDonald all began and ended their stints as manager without looking towards Shankly's long-standing No.1, but the arrival of Bobby Brown was to bring with it a rekindled love for international football.

Consecutive matches for the Reds against Sunderland and Newcastle were penned into Brown's diary and allowed him the opportunity to reassess the likelihood of Tommy returning to the national team. He had been such a crucial part of the iron-hard defence at Liverpool and his performances were finally set to be appreciated again. Although the 2-0 victory over Sunderland saw him as not much more than a spectator, small flashes of brilliance and bravery reminded everyone of the talents the 28-year-old possessed. When the match against Newcastle was postponed, though, Tommy must have felt as though his international chances were cursed.

When a Scottish League XI faced the English equivalent, Jim Cruickshank was given the nod; this meant he was likely to be in the upcoming squad against West Germany. However, the thoughts of Horace Yates in the *Liverpool Daily Post* were: 'If Cruickshank is the best available goalkeeper in Scotland, Liverpool's Lawrence should walk into the national side.' The feeling was growing that Tommy should be back, and when Rankin Grimshaw, a Scotland team selector, was spotted in the crowd for Liverpool's game with QPR just days before the squad was announced for the World Cup qualifier, it began to feel inevitable.

Birmingham City's Jim Herriot had featured in the last World Cup qualifier against Cyprus and it seemed that

Tommy would be competing for a place in the squad with him. However, when it was announced that Birmingham's Second Division match would be played the day before the West Germany match, the chances of a long-awaited return for Tommy increased tenfold. The initial announced pool of 22 players confirmed that both men, alongside Aberdeen's Ernie McGarr, would compete for the starting role in goal. Herriot soon withdrew and, as John Rafferty of *The Scotsman* previewed the team he thought would be selected by Brown, he profiled the returning stopper:

> A long time ago Bobby Brown said that the first qualification for inclusion in the team was experience at the top level of football. He has named an experienced team and only the goalkeeper, Lawrence, has not a long string of caps against his name.
>
> Nobody could, however, describe Tommy Lawrence as inexperienced. For the past five years he has been goalkeeper with Liverpool and all that time he has been working under conditions of strain both in England and on the Continent. He is a well-hardened defender. During these five seasons he has missed only four games for Liverpool.
>
> He has not played in Scotland apart from schools football. He was brought up in Dailly in Ayrshire and went to Liverpool straight from school in 1958.

> He has a wonderful record of consistency. He is, in addition, a big relaxed chap who is upset by nothing and he will have a calming influence on the defence.
>
> He was capped against the Republic of Ireland in 1963, but there is a completely new squad of players now and many he met for the first time on Sunday. He could well be the goalkeeper that Scotland has been seeking for so long. At least he will be safe and unflappable.

Some stories regarding a couple of Scottish players taking a Mercedes out of the car park, enjoying a small joyride around Hamburg, climbing back into bed at 3am after some fun with fire extinguishers in the hotel had spread within the squad. Tommy was rather relieved that preparation for the match in his home nation was a lot more relaxed. Unlike last time, Tommy was now the odd one out with his inexperience being the opposite of his peers. He was part of a rotation team back in 1963 but now the squad selected by Brown was settled and their inexperienced (on the international stage) goalkeeper slotted into a crucial match against the Germans. As well as a settled squad in front of him, 'The Flying Pig' lined up against a team set to be World Cup semi-finalists in 1970 – including a certain Gerd Müller.

Tommy looked back on this match as one of the greatest in his career, not for the scoreline but for the famous striker he came up against. Ryan Murray shared what his grandad thought about the match and one of the greatest goalscorers in the history of the game:

> He was talking about some of the best players that ever scored against him and he was talking about Gerd Müller for West Germany. Word for word, he described how it was and how he should have saved the goal. His memory was shot essentially, but he just remembered everything to do with Liverpool, everything to do with Scotland, everything he did with the football, and mostly what he enjoyed, I think, was people engaging with him.

Being able to experience the Hampden roar for himself as a player, in front of over 115,000 supporters and, although it wasn't the aim before the match, conceding a goal to the best player he ever played against meant that this was a day to never forget for Tommy. His heroic 'Sweeper Keeper' tendencies were on show from the off, as balls were repeatedly chipped over the defence by Franz Beckenbauer, and Tommy had to throw himself at the feet of Müller. The Anfield stopper repeatedly thwarted a formidable foe but the breakthrough came just before the half-time break.

The same duo combined and, with his back to goal, the Bayern Munich man wriggled the ball through the legs of the defender and poked the ball into the corner of the net. If it wasn't for Bobby Murdoch's late stunner that got Scotland back level, then hopes of taking part in the World Cup in Mexico the next year were over. It was a tough match against an impressive opponent but, unlike Tommy's last cap, it certainly couldn't be described as one that had passed him by.

03/05/1969 – Wales vs Scotland

The third instalment, of course, brings with it the now obvious end to the short-lived international experiences of Tommy Lawrence. He was again selected in the pool of 22 for the next matches, beginning with Wales in the British Home Championship. It was clear that the Liverpool man was the preferred option and, for the first time in his career, he was Scotland's No.1.

It ended all too abruptly, though, and a man with a key role in helping drop the curtain on Tommy's time with Scotland was John Toshack. As Gary Jones headed a ball into the box, the trio of Tommy, Toshack and Billy McNeill all tried to get to the bouncing ball first. Both the defender and the striker reached the ball with their boots, while Tommy flew into the face of McNeill and both were emphatically floored. The Scottish trainer ran on to the pitch to treat the two stricken players and it was clear that Tommy was experiencing head and shoulder pain, more than could be healed by the magic sponge that was on offer to him.

As brave as ever, Tommy got back to his feet to take the subsequent goal kick and played on. A matter of seconds later, he flew through the air to catch a Ron Davies header and caught it with impressive ease. Despite the pain he was clearly in, he was willing to put his health on the line for Scotland in just his third appearance. When Toshack launched a half-volley on target, the man between the sticks stood still and looked bemused as it flew past him, no doubt a great goal but there was something amiss. The resilient stopper guarded his net until the half-time whistle but he found himself in a position that hadn't faced him in many years, too injured to play on. The decision was made that Jim Herriot would take to the pitch for the second half and Tommy was taken to hospital with concussion.

It was a terrible time to be injured. Three days later, the Tartan Army were again in action against Northern Ireland, and four days afterwards played England at Wembley. When the World Cup qualifier against Cyprus came around the next week, Tommy was replaced by Herriot in goal and by Ernie McGarr in the squad. This was repeated for all three matches, and a two-week period that should have ended with four caps was cut short through concussion suffered against the Welsh.

Fortunately, it was nothing more sinister. Just nine days after visiting hospital Tommy was representing Liverpool against his counterpart and distant family member Joe

Corrigan's Manchester City. A string of impressive saves in a 1-0 loss showed that the concussion was clearly behind him. Unfortunately, so was his Scotland career. Herriot had staked his claim to the No.1 jersey and the 29-year-old was now the preferred option for the next couple of seasons.

Through no fault of his own, the chance of representing his country was snatched away from Tommy. Although he had every reason to be proud of playing senior international football, it was a chapter in his life that was all too brief. He wasted an opportunity in his first match, where nerves no doubt played a role in a shaky performance, and this then combined with a lack of awareness for his talents from the revolving-door managerial appointments. Add in the ability of a well-respected Bill Brown, then the concussion against Wales (despite an impressive display against West Germany), it meant that nobody wanted to take a chance on Tommy again. He had every reason to hold his head up high but had it not been for the John Toshack collision this could have been a much different story. Ironically, his ever-present and injury-free reputation at Anfield was the opposite of how his career for Scotland ended. Sometimes it's just not meant to be.

New York, Majorca and Blackpool

THE 'WHAT goes on tour, stays on tour' attitude of Shankly's Liverpool team makes this one of the most interesting and difficult chapters. There were many trips that the players went on together in this era, be it pre-season training, European away fixtures, tours before the season began or just general holidays. While many former team-mates of Tommy were more than happy to share all their memories of playing alongside him, some were off-limits, namely the time spent in Majorca.

These holidays were just that: an opportunity for the players to unwind and reflect on the success or heartache of the season before. Shankly didn't want wives or girlfriends to be anywhere near these breaks though; they were strictly for his players and in the hope of building even more togetherness. In fact the manager wasn't the fondest of travel himself, so he would often attend for a couple of days but soon find an excuse to head back home at the earliest opportunity. Chris Lawler reflected on this tradition:

> At the end of every season we used to go to Majorca, we must have done it like six seasons on the run. We would go to the same place and that didn't go down well with the wives because they weren't allowed to go and we would have two weeks away. Let's say there are lots of things that happened, that I can't tell you!

And that's the overarching theme of these mythical trips to Spain. No wives, no family, mostly no manager, and an annual two-week vow of silence where the players could let their hair down. Ian Callaghan added to this mystery:

> We used to go to Majorca because there was a bit of a break at the end of the season. Bill Shankly never came with us, or very rarely, it was always Bob Paisley, Reuben Bennett and usually one of the directors as well. The lads just got a bit of a lecture before you went out, like not to get into trouble or whatever. It was a great bunch of lads, so we used to have a really good time and have a relax. We went quite a few years to Campos Villa in Majorca. You were warned when you were there to be on your best behaviour anyway, because of who you are and the football club. I keep mentioning, it was a great bunch of guys, so nobody got in trouble.

Asked if he was allowed to share any stories from these trips, the club's record appearance holder simply replied: 'No!' This, unsurprisingly, was repeated throughout. 'If I told you the truth, we'd all go to jail!' said Gordon Milne, before adding:

> Those stories were fantastic. The one thing, I don't know how Shankly worked it, but the great thing about that group of players was everybody had different personalities, but they all got on, everybody did. There wasn't a black sheep in the family and they were all different. Chris Lawler and Gerry Byrne were quiet as mice, then you've got the Saint, Big Ron and Willie, the Scots lads, and Tommy was a Scot too but there was a mixture of characters and ability. Yet there were no pretenders. That was obvious because of what the team did on the pitch. So, we wanted to come to Majorca after we'd won something.
>
> That was a reward and it tempted us, we didn't need it but we thought, *Christ, if we can do this, this year, at the end of the season we'll get a week in Majorca again and the boys can get together and go and have some fun!*

Some were a little happier to reveal snippets of information but, in an effort to respect the anonymity of these sacred trips, let's just say that the following was shared by one of Tommy's former team-mates:

Majorca, in the late 1960s, I came down and it must have been around 10am. I thought, *Have I missed the breakfast?* I don't know how it ended up but I must have bumped into Peter Thompson or somebody, and he said, 'They're all in the bar.' I said, 'It's fucking 10am!' and he went, 'I know!' So, I head to the bar and who's leading the fucking parade? Tommy Lawrence! Oh, yeah, fucking right. You know you had to drink, and no halves included, you have to have a fucking pint. 'We don't fucking do halves here!' I said, 'Tommy, it's just gone 10am!'

Shanks would never come. He didn't want to see the lads getting bollocksed and all that every night. The drinking was just really heroic, to be honest! Back in them days it was accepted but it would be unheard of now today. At the end of the day, we were on holiday and it was a break, but Shanks didn't want to watch the lads enjoying themselves.

Tommy and Roger were the linchpins of everything but they were fiercely competitive with Big Ron Yeats and the Saint. When we were all going out at night, you'd get the Jocks and the chameleons, but I would try, at least try, to get everybody together if we could. It would be the Jocks up there and then there's Tommy and Roger and all the others, which I thought, that's not nice. I tried to guide them together.

> And one of them said to me, 'While you're on this trip here, your main job is to fucking get the women in, end of!' What can I say to that? I said, 'I won't let you down, lads, I won't let you down!' I can't tell you everything. There's that much going on, ducking and diving. At the end of the day, we are on holiday and that's why Shanks didn't really want to go. You should be allowed to have a holiday.

George Scott added, 'You wouldn't want to know what went on there!' as he shared images of the players on the beach together. Some of these surviving pictures show a group of lads having fun together. We don't need to delve too far into whatever else may have happened and there are many stories of some of the players wanting to ensure that pictures and stories from these trips stayed under wraps. There were obviously unhappy wives and partners at home, unhappy with Shankly being so fervent in his belief that the players should be allowed a break together without their families.

Tracey, Tommy's daughter, remembered: 'Bill Shankly used to put a Christmas party on for the kids but we weren't encouraged to get together. My mum, I wouldn't say she didn't like Mr Shankly, but she wasn't very happy with him because she said that he used to take the men away every year to Majorca, while the families, we had to stay at home.' Such was the players' trust in their manager, though, that they wouldn't need too much convincing. They were all happy to go away together and face the wrath when they came home.

Some images really aren't for public viewing, whether it be a fashion faux pas or much worse, but if the aim of these jaunts to the sun and sea were to create a togetherness within the Anfield dressing room, it certainly worked. It wasn't just Majorca though. Bobby Thomson shared his memories of other getaways with the lads:

> We went to Nice on the French Riviera. Everybody went to the beach and we all had a good time. It was just a holiday, no training, no nothing, just a holiday. The coaches went with us; somebody had to look after us all! There were never any formal curfews or anything like that. You knew what you had to do. If you were out until 12 or one o'clock in the morning, you got a blast the next morning. You always were supposed to be back at the hotel for nine or ten o'clock.
>
> Shankly would be the one in charge but Bob Paisley was the most familiar with the players. Bob had played for Liverpool himself, and then Joe Fagan, he came in from Manchester City, he was the reserve trainer, but he'd be friendly with the lads too. Paisley was the most fun to be around because Shankly mixed with the players when we were training but once we come away from the training ground, he'd be in his

> office doing all his paperwork. Paisley was the one that used to hang around with us, and Joe Fagan and Reuben Bennett. Stevo [Willie Stevenson] and I used to hang around together but it was a good trip in Nice because all the players got on well together.

Kevin Lewis recalled a trip to Ireland where the players did little more than 'stay in the hotel. We took some clubs out and played a bit of chip and putt on the lawns outside the place but the weather was atrocious!' Ireland was a little further afield than one favourite haunt in Blackpool. Gordon Milne shared:

> We used to go to Blackpool, they used to take us there for three days after a game and we used to enjoy that. I don't think the times that we went to Blackpool, and there were quite a lot over my time playing, that we ever lost at Anfield before – we never went to Blackpool after losing. So, we would play on the Saturday, win, two hours later jump on the bus and off to Blackpool for a couple of nights! All those things were new to us, like going to Majorca was new to us. We weren't innocent but these sort of things had never happened to us before.
>
> Could you imagine going into a dressing room at Anfield today and saying, 'If you win on Saturday, lads, we're going to take you to Blackpool.' Well, you

could imagine how they would look at you. They go to Barbados and Monte Carlo for two days in their private planes and whatever now. If I mention going to Majorca or Blackpool today, my grandkids look at me as if I'm potty, but to us that was amazing, this had never happened before and all of us were in the same boat together. It was fantastic, but it was new, it was new to them and it was new to us.

One of Tommy's final trips abroad was to Sweden, and Jack Whitham remembered how the experienced goalkeeper helped him during one of his first times away from home:

When we were in Sweden for just two weeks, me and Kevin Keegan were new to the club and we were sharing a room together for the fortnight, and on the very last night of that tour, me and Kevin were skint, we didn't have a bean between us. All we could afford was a glass of orange juice that we had to share with two straws. We went to this bar near the hotel where we were staying and we got this glass of orange juice with two straws. On the way back, it was still broad daylight even though it was about 11 o'clock at night, but we bumped into Tommy coming the other way.

Tommy looked at us two and he says, 'Now then, Smithy is looking for you two and he's an angry man.'

> And we said, 'Angry man, why?' He said, 'Because you shunned the lads on the last night of a tour.' We said, 'What are you talking about?' Tommy said, 'On the last night of a tour, everybody goes out together, regardless of whether they're mates or what their differences are.' We said, 'We didn't know, nobody ever told us that!' and he said, 'I'm telling you now! He's an angry man, Smithy, I would keep away from him if I was you!'
>
> So, anyway, me and Kevin go back to the hotel sharpish and went to bed. We get up the next morning, we go down for breakfast and we are terrified, me and Kevin, about what Smith is going to say. We walked downstairs into the breakfast room and we walked straight past Tommy Smith. We never looked at him, but we could see he was glaring at us but he never said anything. If it wasn't for Tommy giving us the warning, we'd have been in big trouble, but it seems like the night's sleep may have calmed Smithy down a bit!

One trip that clearly meant a lot to Tommy, though, was his tour of the US with the rest of the Liverpool squad. Postcards from this trip sent to his mum and dad remained in his possession long after the end of his Anfield heyday. In a series of messages to his family, an insight into his travels across the pond can be used as a diary of his trip:

07/05/1964 – New York

Dear all,

Arrived safely at New York, we fly to Boston to-morrow to play, the weather is about 70° and getting warmer but it has been raining for the last three days,

Love Tom

15/05/1964 – Chicago

Dear all,

We have just left St. Louis for Chicago, I am writing this on the plane. We enjoyed St. Louis very much, I went playing golf with Alan A'Court and a couple of friends that we met here. It was a lot better than New York, write again soon,

Love Tom

17/05/1964 – Chicago

Dear all,

We play the Mexicans [Club de Fútbol Monterrey] today in the Soldier Field, it is where Jack Dempsey fought Gene Tunney [in 1927], it holds 120,000 people seated, after that we leave for New York next day, see you soon,

Love Tom

26/05/1964 – Detroit

Dear all,

We have finally arrived in Detroit, it is a lot better than New York and Chicago but the weather is a lot cooler here, we play to-morrow then fly back to Chicago, write soon,

Tom xx

Although far from a gushing report on American life from Tommy, this was an amazing time for the whole squad. Ian Callaghan also shared his memories: 'I remember it was a bloody long trip! When I say long, I think we were away for about five weeks. I remember in New York that we got invited on *The Ed Sullivan Show*. We all met Dusty Springfield and Gerry and the Pacemakers; they were on the show and we were in the audience. It was a big thing to meet these people and *The Ed Sullivan Show* in them days was massive, it really was, in America. It was a great night.'

There were other examples of Shankly's distaste for foreign travel in his refusal to work on American time, simultaneously wearing a different watch for every time zone in the US and forcing the players to operate on his Liverpool watch. His eccentricities went through the roof and often led to an early flight home. This meant he missed the aforementioned appearance on *The Ed Sullivan Show*. So, when the host asked 'one of the great soccer teams of England, the Liverpool team that won the English league title' to stand up, Tommy followed Ron Yeats and Reuben Bennett in awkwardly accepting the applause of a confused New York crowd.

All these adventures added something different to Tommy's foreign experiences and growth as a man. As Gordon Milne said, a trip to Blackpool was extravagant for all the players of this time and they were experiencing these firsts together. Many disparaging words can be written about the events in Majorca and, whether you think they're stories of Liverpool legends or misbehaving young men, it can at least be agreed that they brought the team together.

Today's players aren't impressed with a club trip abroad, as they can afford more lavish holidays of their own. Often club travels are based around financial gain for the 'brand' as a whole and not just for professional improvement. Although the trip to the US was a way of riding the crest of The Beatles' wave, it provided the players with lifelong memories once more. Each day spent away from their families and sharing rooms gave them a tighter bond and there's no doubt that this contributed to the winning of silverware. Ignoring the success on the pitch, though, to have a squad of players that played together for so long and had such a strong togetherness showed how great a man-manager Shankly was and how perfectly assembled his dressing room was.

Tommy and LFC team-mates celebrate after 1963/64 First Division title win

First Division champions, August 1964

Tommy vs. Leeds United, FA Cup Final, May 1965

Liverpool squad pose with 1965/66 First Division title and 1966 Charity Shield

Tommy Smith, Tommy and Roger Hunt, Wembley, May 1965

Tommy at Anfield, August 1967

Tommy with Tracey and Steve, February 1970

Liverpool squad, Melwood, January 1971

Tommy, Tranmere Rovers, August 1973

Niece Ailsa Tommy and daughter Jayne, 1973

Tommy, Anfield, 1999

Tommy, Shankly's Heroes Night, 2013. Courtesy of Adrian Killen

Scott, Adam, Steve and Tommy Lawrence, Anfield, 2014

Tommy during 2015 BBC interview, via BBC North West Tonight

Tommy and Ian Callaghan, premiere of Shankly: Nature's Fire, *2017*

Watford, Ray Clemence and Leaving Liverpool

THE START of the 1966/67 season was an exciting time for football in England and Liverpool. England had just won the 1966 World Cup, Liverpool were the champions of England and Everton were the FA Cup holders. The traditional curtain-raiser to each season was the Charity Shield, in which the league champions played the FA Cup winners. The match was played at Goodison Park, where both teams could display what they had won the previous season, as well as the Jules Rimet trophy, which was paraded by Roger Hunt and Ray Wilson, the members of the England team who represented Liverpool and Everton.

The match has been described by Derek Dohren as a 'symbolic coronation of a footballing oligarchy', as 63,000 spectators watched this meeting of the two best teams in the country, both from Merseyside. Defining this match as such seems rather over the top, especially for a match that's often deemed no more than a pre-season friendly. Nevertheless, this was a very proud day for the city of Liverpool that showcased the ability of both teams, as well as the friendship and rivalry between them. However, perhaps this match may be best remembered for it being the final time a Shankly team clinched silverware for 2,450 days, after Hunt scored the only goal.

The course of the next seven years marked a considerable period of change for the club and notably for Tommy. His fall from grace was no real reflection on his game, though. This was an ageing squad, and although the goalkeeper is as much to blame as any other member of the team when trophies aren't won, they were all responsible – including Shankly.

The return to the European Cup after winning the league in 1966 brought with it an opportunity of redemption for the losses to Inter Milan and Borussia Dortmund. When Petrolul Ploieşti were drawn as Liverpool's first opponents, hopes were high of swift progression. Shankly had again let a summer pass in which his squad was left untouched, with a young Kenny Dalglish being handed a trial but selecting Celtic as the club he would spend his formative footballing years with. It had been a bumpy start to the campaign and several injuries hampered progression, but a trip to the Romanian champions provided the Reds with a chance to finally stamp their mark on the new season.

A 2-0 victory at Anfield should have marked an easy away leg but Liverpool underestimated the Eastern Europeans in a 3-1 loss, which set up a replay at Heysel. Passage to the next round was secured but it was far from convincing for a team that had aspirations of winning the trophy. Next up was Ajax. The Dutch champions had escaped relegation in the season before their title win and were far from a well-known or respected name in Europe. After seemingly overlooking the challenge of Petrolul Ploieşti, the Reds were set to do the same again. Ajax were some years away from reaching the heights of the trendsetting teams that were to come but their youthful and exciting team was ready to make their mark. Shankly spoke on Dutch television: 'We know of them, but we haven't seen them play,' which highlighted the lack of attention to detail. Ian St John, though, shared how Reuben Bennett had, in fact, gone to watch their European opponents, but when he tried to inform the manager of his thoughts, he was met with the simple reply of 'Reuben, we're not interested in them!'

The December evening in Amsterdam will never be forgotten in the folklore of Liverpool, as much for the thick fog as for the 90 minutes that was to follow. The match was close to being called off but, as the Italian referee Antonio Sbardella claimed that he could see each goal from the halfway line, it was deemed safe to play. Little consideration was given to Tommy Lawrence in goal, though, who was struggling to see what was happening in front of him. He later shared with his grandson, Ryan Murray: 'Ron [Yeats] was shouting, "I can't fucking see the ball, Tommy!" I replied, "I can't fucking see you!" He had to tell me when they entered our half!'

There's no doubt that the conditions were far from ideal but that wouldn't account for the technical lesson that Johan Cruyff and the rest of his team were about to teach the Reds. Passing, moving and scoring for fun, it was 4-0 to the home team before half-time. The English champions were being embarrassed. It's impossible to ignore that the thick fog grew denser as the match went on, and it became impossible for commentators and the supporters to see what was going on. Broadcasting angles were changed to pitch-side cameras, such was the difficulty in vision. Commentary was halted because it was impossible to confirm what was happening. In the brief relief from the torment, in which Shankly's team conceded again, the commentator for the day stated, 'Ajax completely on top, Liverpool looking like a side that is hopeless, hapless, with little will to fight, no determination and apparently not the skill either to get themselves back into this game at all. This must undoubtedly be one of the worst performances Liverpool have given for many, many years.'

It ended 5-1 and Tommy summed up his thoughts:

> We weren't used to being beat, especially not like that. We were champions of England. I'm glad the fog was there because it gave me an excuse to not get

> screamed at by Shanks! Although I couldn't see him [Cruyff] half the time, when I did, I thought the ball was going to end up in the back of the net. Cruyff might have said it was his favourite game of all time … It certainly wasn't mine, I'm glad I never played him again!

Shankly tried to cover up the cracks in his team, blaming the result on the fog and claiming it was so bad that he was able to walk on to the pitch and pass instructions to his players but nobody else could see him because of the terrible weather conditions. 'They're used to the fog,' he claimed, before predicting a 7-0 victory at Anfield. His team (wearing yellow) were unable to beat the Dutch back on Merseyside, though, and a 2-2 draw meant a crushing exit at the second round of the European Cup in a 7-3 aggregate loss.

Many of Liverpool's players were of a similar age and it was finally starting to show. Ron Yeats was losing pace, Tommy was slower coming off his line and the likes of Roger Hunt and Ian St John had started to look fallible. The fans and Shankly didn't want to admit it but the players were ageing. Since spending big when he first took over at the club, there hadn't been much investment in the squad, and although this was likely down to the manager as much as the board, it was having an effect. This defeat against Ajax certainly showed a weakness. Shankly knew that several of his favourites had to start being rotated from the starting line-up.

One man who fell afoul of this was Roger Hunt. He felt Shankly didn't treat his decline from first-team football with respect. The use of substitutions was a very new part of the game, and during an FA Cup fifth-round replay with Leicester City at Anfield in 1969, the boss made only his second-ever tactical substitution, shortly after the 70th minute. Tommy's childhood friend was hooked, and the striker later described that he was 'angry, frustrated and puzzled'. Hunt added, 'I pulled my shirt off and threw it into the dugout before marching straight inside to have a bath.' This was hugely out of character for the soft-spoken forward, but he felt that 'Shankly had lost faith in me … my confidence had been damaged'.

Phil Boersma described events at the club: 'Roger was fucking furious. Absolutely fucking furious after the game. Because Roger was getting taken off at Anfield and that move was probably the knife in the heart for him.' The reaction triggered headlines in the *Daily Express* that resulted in a 'showdown meeting' in which Hunt was prepared to either 'ask to be transferred or quit altogether'. Although fans will recognise that Hunt was past his best, Shankly could have handled this incident with a little more empathy. Fans were torn between a player showing disrespect to their messiah and a love for a forward who had been such a hero for them all.

Similar to this is the story of Ian St John, who recalled the day he was first dropped from Shankly's team: 'Conflicting emotions rise to the surface when I think of [Shankly]. I'm torn between love and hate.' The Scot was dropped by the boss for the first time, for a match at Anfield against Newcastle in 1969. He described it as 'an ambush that came without a hint of warning', because the 31-year-old found out only by reading the team sheet. It was not only that he had lost his place, but it was also that he believed his manager should 'have shown a little courtesy', which upset him more: 'Shankly had let me down.' For a man who was thought of as a great orator and a great people person, this was a bad way to deal with a tender subject. All players must face the realisation that football doesn't last forever, but this wasn't the way to start dismantling a team. The 1965 FA Cup hero was only dropped to the bench but this was a significant moment that marked the beginning of the end of his Anfield career. He had been there for eight years and deserved to have at least been pulled aside and told face to face, rather than reading it on the team sheet.

Fans found this as painful as the players, as they didn't know who to back. This close-knit group of fan favourites was gradually being pulled apart. Shankly knew it had to happen but couldn't bring himself to upset the men he loved so much. The players were confused by a lack of communication and a failure to also accept that their prime playing days were possibly behind them. There was never any hate from the supporters for their manager, though, and as hard as they found it to not see icons like Hunt and St John in the team, it was slowly dawning on everyone that change had to happen.

The players weren't alien to this, though. It was just so difficult in this time as so many of the players were of a similar age. Chris Lawler recalled:

> It's part of your life in football, we used to be on the coach every day, going down to Melwood and the dropping down of players mainly started with Roger Hunt. Someone would ask, 'How old are you now?' to players like Geoff Strong. They'd say '31' and then everyone would be going: 'Oh, fucking hell!' Everyone made a joke of it but it was a bit of a worry for you, when you started to get around the 30 mark. You have to take it professionally.

Tommy, though, was holding his own in this two-season period where the strikers were being rotated. He made 87 appearances and was still the man in goal. However, 1969/70 marked the real campaign of change, and it was clear that it wasn't just a couple of players who were being targeted for rotation but most of the squad. The season started well, with many of the old boys still on the pitch. The Reds were top of the league after ten matches but a 4-1 loss at Anfield to Manchester United showed they had lost their way. Soon they were down to sixth, after a string of draws and defeats, not aided by goals being so hard to come by.

Following a 1-1 draw with West Brom at Anfield in January 1970, Shankly bemoaned the negative approach of the visitors: 'How can you play football against ten full-backs? Tony Brown had one kick in 90 minutes and scored with a shot he didn't hit properly. If he had, Tommy Lawrence would have saved it.' The complaints continued and attention was also drawn towards referee Kevin Howley. As this was the final league match Tommy would play as Shankly's first-choice keeper (ironically against the team that he made his first appearance), it may have been a deflection tactic from his players by the boss, who knew change was edging ever closer.

The truth, however, for Tommy was an injury that would open the door for his swift exit. Ahead of the FA Cup tie against Wrexham, Horace Yates reported for the *Liverpool Daily Post*: 'Lawrence, who was unable to train last week because of a leg injury is still feeling it, and can be listed in the doubtful category. Against that Lawrence has a quick recovery rate and I fancy he will be there to maintain his record of not having missed an FA Cup or League game this season.'

This wasn't the case, though, and Tommy missed his first FA Cup tie since 1962 through a calf injury. Shankly confirmed before the match: 'Tommy is very doubtful at the moment … He was in a worse position this time last week when the injury was more sore than it is now … Trainer Bob Paisley has been working night and day to get him fit … If he doesn't, Ray Clemence is standing by.' At this stage the reliable stopper had missed just four league matches in the past eight years. This was by no means a change that was wanted by either the player or his manager, with every attempt made to allow him to keep up his remarkable FA Cup run, and this shows that Clemence was still very much the back-up at this point.

It has been well publicised just how much Shankly didn't like his players to be injured. Even though it was reported by Mike Charters in the *Liverpool Echo* that the goalkeeper had sustained a 'torn calf muscle', every effort had been made for Tommy to play against the Fourth Division opposition. Horace Yates was quick to laud the incoming option, though: 'I don't think Liverpool will be concerned over the absence of Lawrence. Clemence would have been in many a League side long before this. Only Lawrence's consistency and bravery have prolonged Ray's spell with the reserves.'

The match ended with a comfortable 3-1 victory and Horace Yates recalled one save in particular from the new man in goal: 'Like a spring-heeled cat Clemence covered it, but it was the sort of effort that left spectators debating whether the injured Tommy Lawrence could have got near it.' Tommy would have been fully supportive of the new man filling his duties but it was a performance that sent murmurs of whether the replacement was better than the first choice. Shankly was already noticing that every player he changed for his reserve options was being competently replaced, and when Tommy left hospital the haste with which they had tried to get him fit for the Wrexham clash seemed to somewhat wane. The manager said: 'We are well off for players. Anyone we choose can come in and we are confident they will do a good job.'

Tommy was joined by Peter Thompson in the treatment room and the pair were ruled out of the First Division clash with Nottingham Forest on New Year's Eve. It ended a three-year wait for a league appearance for Clemence, who was eager to take the chance handed to him, much like Tommy had been eight years earlier when he filled in for Jim Furnell. It didn't quite go to plan, though, and a 1-0 defeat meant that when Leicester City were drawn in the FA Cup, Shankly pushed for a return of Tommy and Thompson. The goalkeeper was swiftly declared fit, which meant an immediate reinstatement as No.1. He received, as reported by Chris James in the *Liverpool Echo*, 'a tremendous reception' from the Kop on his return to action in a 0-0 draw that meant a replay at Filbert Street four days later.

Here, Tommy, again as reported by James, 'earned his colours with two magnificent saves – both after Liverpool had taken the lead. First he flung himself to his left to clutch a fierce 20-yard shot from Bobby Roberts and later dived the other way to fist an effort from John Farrington for a corner.' Indeed, Frank O'Farrell, the Leicester manager, said afterwards, 'This was a match which could have easily gone either way. Liverpool's goalkeeper Tommy Lawrence kept them in the game.' It was another performance to signal that Clemence would have to wait for further opportunities, with Liverpool's 2-0 victory lining up Watford in the quarter-finals.

Club secretary Peter Robinson feared Tommy's form could signal a return to Scotland action, as Liverpool's fixture list started to pile up, with league and cup matches before the end of the season. He worried that his best players would be selected for World Cup duty and miss the end of the club campaign, with Tommy still very much one of the best at Anfield. However, there was no indication that the next two matches would be his final swansong.

Tommy's penultimate league match, his last as first-choice keeper, passed without note, a 0-0 draw in icy conditions, which led to Eric Todd writing for *The Guardian*: 'If Lawrence was required to save a shot at all, I confess I did not see it.' By the time First Division football returned for the Reds, Lawrence was frozen out. As soon as title hopes were dashed in these trophyless days, attention turned to the cup competitions instead. When a quarter-final tie against Second Division Watford seemingly paved the way to the semi-finals and another looming trip to Wembley, hopes were restored that this four-year wait for silverware would end.

A young Ray Clemence had been handed his third start of the season in the previous round of the FA Cup, but in an effort to ensure that the Reds booked their place in the semi-finals, Tommy was reinstated in goal. The side blended the youth of Peter Wall (25), Emlyn Hughes (22), Ian Ross (23), Alun Evans (20) and Bobby Graham (25) with the experience of Tommy (29), Geoff Strong (32), Chris Lawler (26), Ron Yeats (32), Ian Callaghan (27) and Ian St John (31). It was a hybrid team of two generations and one that's pivotal in the history of the great team of the 1960s.

The only goal came from Barry Endean on the hour mark, and it went through the hands of Tommy. It was clear that Liverpool's dream of Wembley was just that. If he didn't know before, Shankly was now sure that his two-time league-winning and 1965 FA Cup heroes had gone – it was over.

This was a sudden and unceremonious end to Tommy's career at the top, and it came with little prior warning. The Watford match was the watershed moment but the writing had long been on the wall; however, Shankly had refused to read it. Although change was necessary for the team, it does seem harsh that Tommy was part of the cull. The 'Sweeper Keeper' was not past his best, as the season before this sudden end to action saw him set a league record by conceding only 24 goals in playing all 42 league fixtures. Shankly explained the wholesale changes:

> Although we are not making any revolutionary changes, we have tried to plan for the future. We are trying players out now instead of waiting to next season.
>
> It is essential that we do it now. We have got to have these boys ready for next season and it is no use beginning trying them out next August.
>
> Naturally we were all disappointed with the moderate display we gave at Watford, none more so than I, although I was more disappointed for the 10,000 fans who travelled down to see us.
>
> It will be one of the youngest teams we have ever fielded and these boys have proved themselves in the Central League and now they have got their chance to prove themselves in the big League.

It wasn't a warning to the outgoing experienced heads, it was the end. Out of the FA Cup and ninth in the league meant that the season was all but over in February. Instead of waiting around, Shankly's Liverpool 2.0 was unleashed. The broken record of the same team playing every match every week was over. It was a return to the cutthroat attitude that had seen the likes of Billy Liddell depart the club at the start of the 1960s and it was to be repeated ten years later. Ian Callaghan explained how the changes occurred: 'I remember, when he changed the team. We got beat at Watford and I remember coming in on the Monday and the coaches said, "Don't get changed because we're going on the coach." We went for a friendly game against Blackburn Rovers and we went there because they had changed the team.'

The bigger shock than the cup exit was losing their Monday off after Shankly and Paisley had cooked up their radical plan into the small hours within the realms of the boot room. Asked about why this period was a barren spell for the club, Callaghan added, 'I just don't know, you can't put your finger on it really. Seven seasons without a trophy, looking back, it was a bit of a lull. But, at the end of the day, teams are coming through and the more trophies you win, the more teams want to beat you. I wouldn't say it was a struggle but we just didn't win anything. That was the end of Shankly's first team, basically.'

It was a new era, Shankly seemingly realising that if he didn't start making the tough changes, then a team dumped out the cup by a Second Division team and sitting in no man's land in the table might start looking for a new manager. Nobody wanted a new man in charge but this simply couldn't go on any longer. Watford was a catalyst for change, so a curtain came down on the 60s and on Tommy Lawrence. At the end of the 1969/70 campaign that had seen such change, Bill Shankly spoke with Stan Liversedge of the *Liverpool Echo* and addressed his reasoning for the wholesale changes and plans for the season ahead:

People have come to me and suggested that our F.A. Cup defeat at Watford this past season swayed me into making changes. Believe me. I knew two years ago – even before that – that the time was approaching when I would need to blood new players.

I will confess that, at one stage, I honestly thought the Liverpool line-up which swept all before it in the mid-60s would have lasted longer. Perhaps, after the 1966 League championship success, some complacency crept in. Perhaps time alone has wrought the changes …

Since 1966, I have been preparing myself for the breakup of a great side. At Watford, we were without Tommy Smith and Peter Thompson – although I do not make their absence an excuse for defeat.

But I had already started to ring the changes, before then. The best team in England – a machine which had proved to be skilful, dedicated, fit, persistent and unflinching – but had its heyday …

At one time, there was not a £100,000 player in the country who could have got into my team. Yet it's hard, when you know you have the best and … that it won't always remain so, without changes.

When I called Roger Hunt off the field, in that F.A. cup-tie against Leicester, it was the first public sign that the wind of change was blowing, at Anfield …

> It is always hard to tell a man he isn't playing well – especially a player who has been brilliant in the red shirt of Liverpool. And in the past few months, more than one change has been made.
>
> Cast your mind back … do you recall Gordon Milne, Willie Stevenson? They came before Roger Hunt … and after him, famous names like Ian St. John, Ron Yeats and Tommy Lawrence found they were no longer automatic first-teamers.
>
> Men like these ARE men – they know how a situation is, even if they don't want to accept it … Every one of them is in the middle of a two-year contract, with a two-year option. So no-one will find himself on the outside looking in. If there are departures, the farewell will be amicable, I hope. And advantageous to the man who moves on.

The door was open for aged players to leave if they wanted but Tommy didn't shirk this new challenge. When he returned for pre-season ahead of the next campaign, he showed off his new trim figure. However, he spilled the beans to Chris James of the *Liverpool Echo* about what really happened, in a somewhat unflattering article:

> One of soccer's tubbiest goalkeepers will have a new slim-line look when the season kicks-off in 18 days'

> time. For Tommy Lawrence, the genial Liverpool goalkeeper, has lost more than a stone this summer – by accident.
>
> Tommy – 13st. 12lb. at the beginning of last season – is now all set to challenge for the first-team place he lost to Ray Clemence at the end of last season.
>
> But Tommy has no answer to the mystery of the missing inches. 'They just dropped off me during the summer,' said the player whose figure was always exaggerated by a loose-fitting, floppy jersey.
>
> 'I've played a bit of golf and tennis, but I've not been on a special diet or anything,' he added. 'But I feel great now – better, in fact, than I've felt before. I feel in fine trim and am ready to fight to get my place back.'

There were suggestions in the press that Tommy could still push for a move away from Anfield, with Sam Bartram reporting for *The People*: 'Tommy Lawrence is likely to ask for a transfer this week. The Scottish 'keeper has lost his place in the Liverpool side and plans to discuss his future with Bill Shankly.' This wasn't the case, though. Tommy wasn't leaving just yet but he was very much yesterday's man. For 1970/71, this new decade and new era was ready for a new line-up. Larry Lloyd, Brian Hall, John Toshack, Alec Lindsey, Steve Heighway and one man in particular – Ray Clemence – were the new Liverpool. At the end of the campaign Bill Shankly stood on the steps of St George's Hall after the FA Cup Final defeat to Arsenal and inspired the next generation of fans and players, all while Tommy was plotting his exit to Tranmere Rovers.

* * *

Ray Clemence has somewhat been painted as the bad guy for taking the place of Tommy but that was never the case. The two were great friends, had huge respect for each other and it's fair to say that Shankly couldn't have picked a better player and man to take over from his 'Flying Pig'. It seems only right that we allow one hugely important figure to voice their opinion on events and speaking with LFCTV, the England international explained how his move to Liverpool came about:

> My summer job was working on the deck chairs in Skegness, I was dishing the deck chairs out and all of a sudden, somebody came down from the council and said, 'We've had a phone call from your mother, saying Scunthorpe have been on the phone, they've agreed a fee with Liverpool – do you want to go?' I got on my bike, went back to my house, went back to Scunthorpe and said, 'Yeah, I'd love to have the opportunity.'
>
> The following day, I came across in the chairman's Rolls-Royce to Liverpool to meet the one and only

> Bill Shankly. He said, 'We've watched you a lot, son. We're impressed with what we've seen, we think you could be in the big team. We've got Tommy Lawrence here, Tommy's past his best, he's now 30 years of age, and if you keep improving you'll be in the team within six months.'
>
> I came back for pre-season training and within a week I found out that Tommy Lawrence wasn't past his best, wasn't 30 years of age, he was 27 years of age, at the peak of his career and I had to wait two and a half years to get in the team! He did kid me a little bit but it was worth the wait!

Shankly had used his oratory skills to his advantage once again and tied down one of the most impressive young stoppers in the game. This meant that whenever Tommy did show any sign of weakness, the right man was already at the club to fill his boots. Time in the reserves would mould Ray into the type of player the club wanted, which came from coaching by the many influential members of Shankly's staff, and from Tommy himself.

> Tommy was playing exceptionally well so, quite rightly, it was impossible for me to get a chance in that team. I came knowing I was No.2, pushing to be No.1 and lucky that I was in a great reserve team.

> We won the Central League six years on the bounce and I was part of that for my three years with the reserves. I watched the first team whenever I could and learned from Tommy Lawrence. Not in terms of verbally but watched him play.
>
> At that time, Liverpool pushed up the field, Tommy Lawrence was the very first sweeper keeper and I watched his positioning and what he did. He was the best one-vs-one goalkeeper I'd ever seen at that time. I looked at what he did so that whenever the opportunity finally came, I was ready for it.
>
> When I became a regular, it was the year that Liverpool got beat by Watford down at Vicarage Road. They got beat 1-0 in the quarter-final of the FA Cup and after that Bill Shankly made the decision to take the heart out of the middle of the Liverpool team and put myself, Larry Lloyd and Doug Livermore into the team.

Ray was in and never looked back. In the words of Ian Callaghan, 'he became one of the, if not the, greatest goalkeepers Liverpool have ever had – without doubt. So, that obviously made it easier for Tommy to be replaced.' In the next 11 years, Ray won five league titles, three European Cups, the FA Cup, two UEFA Cups, the League Cup, the

European Super Cup and is held by many as the greatest to have ever played in goal for Liverpool.

If we can fast-forward a little, the pair reunited in later years when Tommy attended a legends evening and his grandson Ryan shared the story from there:

> When we told him, 'Ray Clemence is coming, you know,' his eyes shot up and he went around telling everyone, he spent ages saying it, saying his best mate, Ray Clemence is coming. He used to call a few people his best mate, Roger Hunt and Ray Clemence specifically were the people who he called his best mate the most though.
>
> His eyes shot up when Ray Clemence arrived from London and the biggest hug you've ever seen. He was talking about Ray, talking about how he should have been No.1 way before he had the chance to do it, how great he was, his admiration for him, admiration for the fact that Ray always respected him as a teacher – it was amazing.

This respect they had for each other was enduring. If any praise came the way of Ray in front of Tommy, the joke would always be, 'I taught him everything he knew!' Even though Ray Clemence was the man who ended Tommy's career just short of the ten years needed for a testimonial, and the terrible consequences that came from this in the future, there was nothing but love and admiration from Tommy – something that was clearly reciprocated.

* * *

Tommy simply slipped into the role that Ray Clemence had left vacant and became part of a dominant reserve team. Jack Whitham played alongside the Scot and explained his role at the club:

> We were a million miles too good for the rest of that league, we won the Central League in that year, 70/71, they won it again the following year. Roy Evans was captain of the reserve team at that time and they seemed to win the Central League every year.
>
> We had too many good players in the reserve team for the rest of the league. I remember against Blackburn Rovers and I looked at our squad, it was phenomenal. It was Tommy Lawrence in goal, Ron Yeats was playing, Ian St John, Bobby Graham, Alun Evans, Peter Thompson on the left wing, it was ridiculous. It was like a First Division squad at that time, just playing for the reserves. We had a great team before they dropped down and just swapped Ray Clemence for Tommy, Larry Lloyd for Ronnie Yeats, Steve Heighway for Peter Thompson and a few months later Kevin Keegan. Top players

> for Liverpool in the late 60s were now playing for Liverpool Reserves, so we had a brilliant side.

As much as the former first-teamers were frustrated and many were plotting their exit in search of first-team football, the respect for their manager and team-mates meant that everything remained convivial within the dressing room and in training. If anything, it was too friendly, Whitham recalling another story:

> Shanks did not encourage the same camaraderie in the dressing room or closeness of individuals that they encouraged at other clubs. Shanks told me the reason for that, whether he told the other lads, I don't know, but he called me into the office one day and he said, 'I understand you're playing tennis every day with Toshack.' That was during the summer. And I said, 'Yeah, we do play, gaffer, yes. I played for Lancashire, he used to play for Glamorgan. We joined Formby Tennis Club and we're playing a lot.'
>
> He says, 'Don't play tennis with Toshack, son,' and I said, 'Why is that?' He said, 'You don't want to get too friendly with people who you're vying for a position with.' And I said, 'Well, I don't play target man, gaffer, I'm not a centre-forward,' and he said, 'No, but some day you might be wanting each

other's spot in the side, son. It's not a good idea to be too friendly with somebody who you might want their place.'

Now, I don't know if that was endemic in the rest of the squad, that he didn't want two full-backs being too friendly. He wasn't there to encourage you to be over-friendly with other people, particularly with people in your position. Tommy won't have a bad word for anybody, so I don't know whether Shanks ever said that at all to him and Ray. They seemed to get on, particularly in training, because goalkeepers had their own routine. They seemed to get on like a house on fire them two. I don't know of anything that affected Tommy, he was just that laid-back. I don't think anybody or anything was going to really upset Tommy, he probably just accepted it and he taught Ray a lot.

After Tommy spent the rest of the 1969/70 season in the reserves, this continued for 1970/71 too, other than a place on the enlarged benches that were able to be used in the 13th and final iteration of the European Inter-Cities Fairs Cup. It was this competition that paved the way for Tommy to make one final appearance for the club he had spent his entire adult life with. Amid the two legs of the semi-final against Leeds United, Shankly had a radical idea. Between the first leg at Anfield and the second at Elland Road, the Reds had to play six times in a 14-day period. The last match before the second leg was away to Manchester City, just two days before meeting Leeds, so wholesale changes were made. It was written in the *Runcorn Weekly News*:

> Liverpool and Manchester City have both laid themselves wide open to league action after fielding totally understrength teams for their First Division clash at Maine Road on Monday night. But it is doubtful if either Bill Shankly or Joe Mercer will be losing any sleep over the subject. With vital games imminent for both teams, the respective managers just couldn't take the chance of getting key players injured in a game of no importance. It sums up the whole farcical fixtures system which demands the impossible from top class clubs who are expected to field the same team for up to three games in a week.
>
> Bill Shankly offered his protest in the only way he could – by fielding his full Central League side. But with players of the calibre of Bobby Graham, Ron Yeats, Tommy Lawrence, Alun Evans and John McLaughlin on the team sheet, can anyone call this a reserve team? What it does is emphasise the importance of a large first team pool. A manager must be able to call on 22 players in this day and

> age of congested fixtures if he hopes to achieve any measure of success. The league must appreciate the drain and demand expected of top class players and use their common sense when and if they judge both Liverpool and City.

Even if this was just a protest from Shankly, it allowed some the opportunity to play one final time for the 'big team'. It was a last appearance for Liverpool for Chris Fagan, Steve Arnold, Tommy Lawrence and a penultimate one for Ron Yeats. It broke up Ray Clemence's ever-present record that season too, and meant that he couldn't take the record away from Tommy of only conceding 24 goals while playing an entire league campaign. Fewer than 18,000 supporters attended Maine Road to watch two second-string teams, with 20 changes made collectively from the teams that were predicted in the matchday programme. Both line-ups were read out twice to supporters, as if to allow everyone the opportunity to get their head around who was playing.

It wasn't the perfect end for Tommy, though, when, as reported by Paul Wilcox in *The Guardian*, 'City however, somewhat fortunately, were awarded a penalty in the eightieth minute when Lawrence was adjudged to have illegally ended a good run by Francis Carrodus and Stephen Carter scored his first League goal from the spot.' It ended 2-2 and Liverpool were handed a Football League record fine of £7,500 for fielding the weakened team. This was deemed a calculated risk ahead of a European semi-final with Leeds and looming FA Cup Final against Arsenal. However, seeing as both matches were lost, it may not have been a gamble that paid off.

Tommy played with 41 different players during his illustrious first-team Liverpool career and five new ones were in this final match – including Roy Evans. The man who would go on to manage the Reds only made 11 appearances for the first team but was a stalwart of the persistently successful reserve team that he captained with distinction. This match at Maine Road was his ninth for the first team and he shared his memories of it:

> We didn't understand why the club was given a fine. We were made up to get a chance to play in the first team, just delighted with it really, but the club was punished. Obviously, you weren't a first-team player, but you get a chance and you're just hoping you can kick on from there. I think it was about Shanks playing young players in the first team and because people are paying top money to watch top games there was some backlash.
>
> If you're going to play young players, I think you've got to play maybe one or two in the first team at a time and never five or six, because otherwise you may

> as well just be playing for the reserve team. There was a lot of younger players and the likes of Tommy, who was obviously right at the end of his career then. Tommy was one of those guys, he was always there, always helpful to everybody – whether you're a young lad or you're one of the top players.

Another experiencing a first match with Tommy was Jack Whitham:

> That's the only game I played with Tommy. All the others I played with him would be in the reserves or on tour with him. It was a last-minute decision to play that reserve team. You just get out and you do what everybody is doing, to try and say, 'Well, okay, it's a first-team game. I'm not in the first team but if I make a good impression, I might then break into the first team.' You just get out there and you do your best, hoping to get a place in the team when he picks the proper team. You had to be prepared at Liverpool, it was a totally different way of doing things. You didn't know the team until you go in the dressing room, on the day of the game.

But that was the end, a pointless Monday night match in front of a small crowd, after which the club accepted a fine for fielding a weakened team and Tommy conceded a penalty that was then scored past him. Less than a month before his 31st birthday it was clear that Tommy's days were numbered. He was used to playing at the highest level and had never let the club down. Part of a drastic decision from Shankly to overhaul his team, 'The Flying Pig' had his wings clipped. After a season and a half with the reserves, barring sitting on the bench for European ties and the last dance against Man City, it was time to look for pastures new. No bad blood, no animosity, no fairy-tale ending, just a natural end to a glittering career at the top, but one that was a couple of years short of securing a nest egg that would have made the rest of his life so much easier.

Tranmere, Chorley and Daten

THE SUMMER before the 1971/72 season, other than seeing Tommy and Ron Yeats winning the Liverpool Meat Traders' Golf Society invitation day, saw 'The Flying Pig' still a Liverpool player, but his head was soon to be turned. Such was the level of the reserves, who had won the Central League for the past three seasons on the bounce, they were in high demand for pre-season friendlies and travelled across the Mersey to play against Tranmere Rovers. Tommy was part of the first-team squad for the Charity Shield against Leicester City but only as emergency cover for Ray Clemence, so it was very clear that he would remain No.2. There was a running joke that Tommy would pretend to trip Ray up whenever he was near some stairs so he could get back into the team, but he knew his role and was never anything but fully supportive of Ray.

Tommy began the season with the reserves but by the end of September headlines were being written about him. Mike Charters reported for the *Liverpool Echo*: 'Tranmere Rovers clutched a lifeline to-day to help them in their financial crisis by completing a goalkeeper deal with Liverpool – Frankie Lane moves to Anfield, Tommy Lawrence to Prenton Park, plus a £15,000 fee for Rovers.'

The Reds had seen how cash-strapped the club from the Wirral were during the pre-season game against the reserves. With 31-year-old Tommy ageing and Tranmere's best player being their keeper, it seemed like the perfect opportunity to add cover for Ray Clemence with a younger option. Frankie Lane, then 23, was catching the attention of several First Division suitors and the chance to make the step up to such a prestigious club that was very close to home made it a no-brainer. To have Tommy involved in the deal made great sense for Tranmere too, as they would get a hugely experienced player who also wouldn't need to relocate. For Tommy it would be the opportunity to play first-team football – even if it was in the Third Division. To be given a £15,000 boost and receive a hugely talented man in goal made perfect sense for everyone involved and helped solve some financial concerns for Tranmere.

The move was confirmed as Tranmere officials travelled to Anfield on the evening of Liverpool's European clash with Servette. The Reds had qualified for Europe as FA Cup runners-up as Arsenal had won the double the previous season. Neither player was aware of what was happening until the next day in training when they were swiftly sent in the opposite direction through the Birkenhead tunnel. The deal was completed so swiftly that Tommy was eligible for Tranmere's weekend clash with Halifax. The *Liverpool Echo* report continued: 'The twist in the deal was that Lawrence went to Tranmere on loan – at the direct request of Mr. Shankly.'

Although this deal was completed swiftly enough for Tommy and Frankie to play for their new clubs immediately, the deadline for new players to be registered in European competition had passed. Therefore, Liverpool's looming Cup Winners' Cup fixtures would see no experienced back-up option on the bench to add cover for Ray Clemence. New players couldn't be added to the squad until the quarter-final stage, so it was agreed that Tommy's first three months at Prenton Park would see him allowed to return to be a substitute for the Reds for their European clashes. It was an unusual agreement but one that showed some impressive foresight from Bill Shankly and a clear appreciation of the talents of the man they were allowing to leave the club.

Tranmere were thrilled with the move, general manager David Russell saying, 'We have sold a very good goalkeeper in Lane, obtained another one in Lawrence, who can give us years of fine service.' In fact, there was such respect for what was going on at Liverpool that on the same day it was announced that the Wirral club had approached Ron Yeats to not only join the club but be a player-coach. This was to mark the start of a Liverpool renaissance at Tranmere.

Tranmere's team manager Jackie Wright, who was probably not too enthusiastic to see the Yeats links, was also excited to have Tommy in his team and knew that his presence would help 18-year-old reserve goalkeeper Dickie Johnson develop into an even better player, ensuring he would be ready to take the No.1 shirt whenever it became available in the future. It was also reported by Jim Mansell in the *Liverpool Echo*: 'Rovers have already agreed that [Lawrence] should have a testimonial match at the appropriate time. Mr. Shankly was unable to grant Lawrence this match so Rovers stepped in to help out.'

Testimonials, for anyone unaware, were commonplace in those days. Clubs offered players a testimonial match after ten years' service. It still exists in the modern game but far less frequently. Firstly, there's a lot less loyalty nowadays, and secondly, there's less financial need for players. Back in Tommy's era, the money raised from ticket sales and whatever else was associated with the day would be given to the player whose career was being celebrated. This wasn't a time when a footballer retired and had a throne of money to sit on. In fact, many would immediately return to work. Although wages were on the rise for the players, compared to those from ten to 20 years before, it was still not much more than the average working man. Therefore, a testimonial would be a huge help in bridging the gap between playing football and entering working life.

Tommy was unfortunate in this case. Despite joining Liverpool in 1957, he didn't make his first-team debut until 1962, so when he departed in 1971, 58 days before the start of 1972, he had only spent nine years at Anfield in the first team and wasn't eligible for this financial and sentimental goodbye. His Reds career actually spanned 14 years, from reserves, to first team, then back to the reserves, but this didn't qualify him. Fortunately, it appeared that Tranmere were likely to offer him this reward 'at the appropriate time'. Yet it would no doubt gain less attention and thus financial reward if it was a Third Division club rather than Shankly's Liverpool. With the likes of Gerry Byrne, Roger Hunt, Ian St John, Ron Yeats, Tommy Smith, Ian Callaghan, Peter Thompson, Chris Lawler, Emlyn Hughes, Ray Clemence, Steve Heighway, Kevin Keegan and Bill Shankly rewarded with testimonials, it's criminal that Tommy wasn't.

At Tranmere Tommy was immediately thrust back into the limelight, but when he conceded two goals in the opening 15 minutes of his debut away to Halifax, it became clear that he was no longer at the pinnacle of his game. In front of fewer than 5,000 spectators, Rovers fought back to level the score but ultimately succumbed to a late goal. Tommy was soon to realise that he was somewhat of an anomaly in that he was happy to drop down the divisions. It was becoming the norm to see bigger clubs poaching talent from the lower leagues, with clubs forced to sell through financial hardship, thus the quality of the Third and Fourth Divisions was reduced, and it became less appealing to play for a club several divisions below. However, defeating Brighton in his home debut at Prenton Park must have helped ease some initial concerns for Tommy about whether he had made the wrong move.

The next fixture saw rotation in goal as Dickie Johnson replaced Tommy for the Liverpool Senior Cup semi-final against Southport. Given the fact that the man who was still only on loan at the club would soon be back on the bench at Anfield, it was important to bed the 18-year-old into the squad and allow him the opportunity to play more minutes. The chance for the teenager to share a training pitch with a two-time league winner, FA Cup winner and Scottish international was huge and he shared some of his memories of being Tommy's team-mate:

> I've just got this overwhelming picture of Tommy being such a nice fella. In training he was so supportive to me. I remember watching him in training and being amazed by his quality because everything came so easily to Tommy.
>
> I remember when Tranmere played Stoke in the FA Cup, there was 24,000 at Tranmere and they were

hanging from the floodlights, it was just mayhem. I remember I was sitting in the dugout. I was a young lad. I was with Tommy a little bit before the game and I just remember thinking, *You're so calm!* I was petrified as a young lad but he was just so calm, laughing and joking with the rest of the lads. He sure seemed very senior to me then. I know he'd played in a lot bigger games obviously for Liverpool, but he was just so calm.

He was very supportive. I played the second half at Anfield in Ron Yeats's testimonial game. It was against Celtic and there was a massive Celtic away support. Tommy played the first half because Ray Clemence was away with England. Ron Yeats had taken me, Tommy and a couple of other young lads over there from Tranmere, me and Tommy played a half each. Second half was at the Anfield Road End in front of all these Celtic fans. It was absolutely chocker with Celtic fans. There was no problem, they were all very vocal, shall we say, and again I was a little bit nervous. But Tommy was that calming influence to me, he would say, 'Just go out and concentrate on the game, don't worry about them, you'll be fine.' He was always very supportive and that's the lasting memory I've got of Tommy, so supportive and genuinely a nice man.

Tommy took his mentoring role seriously, which again shows how much of a positive influence he was on his team-mates; there was genuinely not one person involved in this book who had anything negative to say about him as a man. Within a matter of weeks of initially signing for the club though, Tommy was back at Anfield for their clash with Bayern Munich.

Tranmere had a rare Wednesday match themselves, against Aston Villa, so Johnson was back in goal. Tommy's return to his former home passed without any fanfare, and the Reds again missed the opportunity to thank Tommy for his years of excellent service.

A potential shock move for Roger Hunt hit the press the following day, linking him with swapping Bolton for Tranmere. Tommy was described by Horace Yates, in the *Liverpool Daily Post* as a 'trump card' in possible negotiations. Roger had announced he would retire at the end of the season, though, and saw no reason to move to the Wirral, even though he had lost his place in Bolton's first-team squad. This dramatic and no-doubt emotional reunion of the Culcheth duo would have been the perfect way to see out this tale but sadly it never came to fruition.

Tommy was soon boarding the plane with Shankly's team to watch them face Gerd Müller and his Bayern team-mates in what was his final involvement in any Liverpool match. There was finally some attention paid to the fact that this 14-year relationship was about to end, with Roger Kelly writing for the *Daily Post*:

> Although he is a hardened professional, it is a sentimental journey for Lawrence, and this likeable Scotsman freely admits he will feel twinges of sorrow when he finally steps off the aircraft back at Liverpool Airport tomorrow.
>
> He was at Melwood on Monday and yesterday, training with his former team mates who are just as aware that a 14-year association is coming to an end.
>
> 'It's your swan song,' one player reminded him in the dressing room.
>
> 'Perhaps I'll come on in Munich as a substitute and save a penalty. That would be a sensational finale,' responded the jovial Lawrence.

There was no moment of unlikely heroics from the standby. It ended in a 3-1 defeat and 'The Flying Pig' watched on as his old foe Müller beat Clemence twice in the space of two minutes. Although his departure could have been handled better, Tommy was afforded the rare opportunity of knowing this was the end for him at Liverpool. Given how quick his transfer was to Tranmere, it was normal for players to leave a club promptly, with little time to do more than throw the belongings from their locker into a bin bag, before driving directly to their new club. The flight back from Munich at least allowed those players that Tommy had spent so many years playing alongside to say goodbye. Radio presenters joined for the trip too and interviews were held to mark this momentous occasion of the end of Tommy's career as a Red.

It seemed to inspire Tommy to make a name for himself at Tranmere, returning with a fine performance against York, keeping a clean sheet in front of his supporters. Liverpool chairman Peter Robinson was spotted in the crowd but this was only to finalise the paperwork that ended the loan deal. It meant that Tommy was now officially part of the Super White Army. Another man set to join him was Ron Yeats. On the eve of 1972, the Scot was announced as player-assistant manager on the Wirral and spoke about joining his former team-mate: 'If we can win as much together at Tranmere as we did at Liverpool, we won't be complaining!'

Within four months Yeats took the top job from Jackie Wright, which wasn't too much of a surprise, given how public he had been with his wishes to become a manager. Seeking an opportunity to benefit from Liverpool being unable to keep hold of their most experienced players and converting them into coaches at Melwood, Tranmere pounced. Tommy opened the door, Yeats was next and was now the boss. Where Shankly had launched Liverpool 2.0 at the start of the 1970s, it seemed that Rovers were now trying their best to do the same. First came Kit Fagan, son of Joe, a full-back who had failed to make an impact during his limited first-team opportunities. He was joined by fellow youngster Eddie Flood. Next was Ian St John, before Willie Stevenson also made the move back to Merseyside. Bobby Graham was loaned from Coventry City as well, and it was clear that Yeats had a plan of restoring the glory days of Anfield at Prenton Park.

Despite these good intentions and the success that these players had with both the first team and reserves for Liverpool, Yeats was soon to discover what Shankly had several years before. Signing experienced players was great but Prenton Park became somewhat of a retirement home for these declining talents. This was an already average Third Division team, and it wasn't improved by an inexperienced manager using overly experienced players. Perhaps if Yeats had his time at Prenton Park again he would have spent more time nurturing talents such as Dickie Johnson, who commented on the Scot's managerial style:

> As a manager, I can remember Ron. The thing we used to say about him was after training on a Friday, or a Thursday, because Tranmere used to play a lot of the games on a Friday night at this time. He picked the team. Ron Yeats, the morning of every game, or at the end of the previous day, he'd get all the lads in and he'd always tell a joke. You always used to hear him tell jokes to the whole changing room and the

> story went that whoever laughed the loudest got in the team! We'd be rolling about laughing, just hoping he'd give us the nod the next day!

Willie Stevenson also had his say on getting the old gang back together at Prenton Park: 'Well, I think to be honest, most of us felt we were lucky to still be playing. We were no spring chickens, we were all 34 and 35. We had already had our careers, to be honest with you, but we loved it. It was great being back together.' At the very least, it was wholesome for Tommy to rekindle old friendships from his glory days at Anfield. Add this to a bond with Syd Farrimond, who had joined from Bolton, and a rekindled friendship with Roger Hunt in Culcheth after his retirement.

After Yeats taking charge of his first match in January, Rovers ended the season in 20th position. By time his relationship with Tranmere ended in April 1975, they were on the brink of relegation to the fourth tier – something new boss John King was unable to reverse. It was an unsuccessful introduction to senior management for Yeats and certainly didn't go how any of the former Reds had hoped. One member of this team was Ray Mathias, and he revealed more about Tommy's role at the club at this time and during training:

> What I can remember just of Tommy, he was a very down-to-earth fella, despite all the achievements. He

was just another person and that's the way he treated everybody else as well, with respect.

We went training one day and Tommy was a smoker. In his car he had all stumps all over the mats, not over the carpets but on the mat. He still lived in Warrington and drove in every day, but that was Tommy, that was him really, it was the way he was. He was probably one of the quickest people to get changed from his training kit and back into his normal clothes when he had finished his training. He was in and out quicker than anyone to get back home because he was a homely sort of gentleman and he loved a game of golf. He'd rush off to get to the golf course with his golf partner Roger Hunt.

Some of the comedy stories were when we used to go training at a place called Storeton Woods. You did circuits around the woods and we used to be in about three groups, and the circuits were quite hard. We would start off in these groups and each would go off at different times and they'd all be running at the same time. But the group that Tommy was in, Tommy would be missing out for a lap. So, everybody's saying, 'Where's Tommy?' as they were running along. Anyway, next minute, Tommy is back in the group again when you get round for another lap. So, he's obviously missed a lap and jumped out after he's been hiding in the trees and joined in for the last lap!

It seemed that Tommy was taking some liberties with his old mate in charge. Whereas he had previously hidden his smoking and drinking habits from those inside his football circle, for Tranmere team-mates to notice cigarette butts in the car meant things had changed. His son Steve explained how, at his worst, his dad smoked 40 each day. Thankfully this smoking habit was replaced with Polo mints after retiring, but this didn't end too well as he needed to have teeth removed because of how many mints he was now sucking!

He also wasn't too fond of the running requests. Dick Johnson recalled the pair of them also hating running along Moreton beach, but there were fewer trees there to hide from watching eyes! Although a slightly rotund figure was part of his image, there was never a hint from anyone at Liverpool that anything but 100 per cent was given in training. With a poor team, ageing players, an inexperienced manager and less motivation within training, it was clear that the end was nigh for Tommy. Nobody in this era was an athlete like we see in the game today, especially within the Third Division. However, this lack of focus on things that can make a big difference to how you play meant that as his body began to fail him the Scot was doing the same to it. Johnson added: 'I don't think he had anything to prove. I don't think he was putting everything into the training but I don't think he had to because his ability saw him through, his ability and his experience.'

There were still flashes of brilliance though. Take one save against Charlton in 1972 that Tommy described: 'I suppose it must be among the best saves I've ever made. Those point-blank volleys are almost impossible to stop if the forward hits them right, but I dived and pushed it away.'

To play 82 matches during the 71/72 and 72/73 campaigns shows that Tommy was still proving to be an ever-dependable option in goal. He could have easily looked down his nose at the challenge of playing in the third tier but that was never the case and not what ultimately held him back. Damaging knee ligaments in March 1973, though, signalled a return to action for Dick Johnson, who was eagerly awaiting an opportunity to shine. It was the most long-term concern of Tommy's career. Despite several returns to the first team, he just couldn't fully shake this knee injury off. When Ronnie Moran's Liverpool Reserves faced Tranmere in the Liverpool Senior Cup Final, Tommy again couldn't feature and missed out on the chance to play against a Liverpool team for the first time.

By the time pre-season for 1973/74 came around, Tommy was back in the team but showing signs that his 33-year-old body was now deteriorating. Reports such as 'Goalkeeper Tommy Lawrence had some good moments, yet could perhaps be faulted for not moving quicker to prevent the equaliser' became more frequent. He was still pulling off fine saves and was one of the star players within the Tranmere team but injuries had again occurred by September of the new season. Although he had started the campaign with six straight clean sheets, he was set to sit out again.

When he was finally fit again two months later, Yeats had seen enough in Dickie Johnson to keep him in position as the No.1. Again, it wasn't the performance level that had seen Tommy lose his place but the emergence of a young talent who took his chance when the door opened. It was somewhat of a yo-yo season, with both keepers impressing, maintaining their role in goal, picking up an injury, allowing the other back in and then waiting for injury to hit again. Yeats was blessed to have two strong options and the pair were more than happy to share the role, such was the respect that they had for each other. Tommy fought his way back in by December but was injured again in January 1974. The talent was still there but the body's reliability was not.

As the season edged to its close, Tommy continued to watch from the sidelines. New Brighton approached Tranmere about Tommy's possible signing but Yeats wasn't ready to let his old mate leave just yet. This was to come at the end of the season, however, when it was confirmed by the club that they were to allow Tommy to leave on a free transfer – with Gordon West filling his role on the Wirral. The former Everton keeper was known for his ability to come off his line, something the Goodison faithful were as uneasy with as the Anfield fans when they first watched their No.1 come running off his line. It was another first, the first-ever sweeper keeper was now an unwanted man in the third tier. Out of loyalty, Yeats allowed the stopper to be part of the club tour to Spain but he was the one who had to tell him that he was no longer a wanted man on the Wirral. Tommy was now faced with a decision: retirement or look for another club.

Charles Lambert wrote in the *Liverpool Echo*:

> Lawrence learned this week that he was being given a free transfer by Third Division Tranmere Rovers and that means he must wait to see if any other League clubs are in need of a veteran goalkeeper, or take a job and turn out for a non-league side … or pack up altogether. Whatever decision Tommy Lawrence takes, it will seem a million miles from that day in 1965 when Liverpool won the cup for the first time.

After a month in limbo – although he trained with Tranmere and took part in Ron Yeats's testimonial (the Wirral club never followed up with an offer of one for Tommy) – a new club was found. In August 1974 it was announced that he would join Cheshire League club Chorley. The 33-year-old was immediately thrust into action again but a mistake against New Brighton on his debut meant a 3-1 loss and an opportunity to rue Ron Yeats's decision to not allow his move to that day's opponents a few months earlier.

Meanwhile, Yeats's Liverpool experiment at Tranmere had failed and was being swiftly dismantled. The end of Tommy's playing days were now far away from the glare of an interested audience too. He played in goal for the Magpies during the 1974/75 campaign, until the same story of his former clubs played out. Tony McMahon, who would go on to be known as a legendary shot stopper at Victory Park, soon won the No.1 jersey and never looked back.

Tommy continued an involvement with Liverpool by partaking in the many testimonials of his former team-mates, although still never given a hint of being rewarded himself. He and Roger Hunt would often be seen reunited on the pitch, such as taking part in a testimonial at Warrington Town, where three players were rewarded for 36 collective years of service in 1975. There were even some punditry appearances where Tommy helped judge a 'Save of the Month' competition for Granada's *Kick-Off*, appearing alongside ex-Manchester United man Carlo Sartori.

It was an ending that didn't befit Tommy's career. His good nature meant that he never kicked up a fuss when he lost his place to Ray Clemence and Dickie Johnson. His performances never really warranted his removal from either team but perhaps him being such a nice man worked against him. Shankly and Yeats were aware that they wouldn't receive any backlash from 'The Flying Pig' when they dropped him, and that's how it worked out. He had every reason to feel aggrieved but instead he played one final season with Chorley and left without any fanfare. He was owed a testimonial from Liverpool, promised one by Tranmere and even played in many for other players, but this opportunity was never handed to him. The end of his playing career passed without so much as a mention from anyone. The harsh reality of looking for a job for the first time since his stint as an office clerk on Hob Hey Lane for Joseph Lythgoe, son of the man who had provided Tommy's parents with their employment in Culcheth, was upon him.

* * *

That may be the end of the 'ordinary' career of Tommy but there was one more adventure into competitive football, less than half a mile from The Pack Horse. This comes with a short history lesson too. In 1946, the Ministry of Supply formed its Division of Atomic Energy with the task of generating electricity. Those working on the project were based in Culcheth. Frustrated by a lack of recreational facilities, the workers asked for investment in the local area so that they had something to do. This led to the founding of the Division of Atomic Energy Club. Over time the rather lengthy name was colloquially shortened to DATEN (Department ATomic ENergy). This name is now part and parcel of Culcheth life, with Daten Football Club still playing today, and it also just so happened to be based around the corner from Tommy's house.

Still in love with the game, Tommy relished the opportunity to watch football at any level. With the club being so close to his house, The Pack Horse and having its own bar too, there were always plenty of reasons to spend time there. Tommy's son Steve joined the club in his late teens, so it was commonplace in the early 1980s to see the former Scotland international supporting his lad. Never one to scream abuse at officials, Tommy would stand alone, watching from afar but, with him being such a local celebrity, everyone knew who he was.

Mike Henshall, former secretary, and Trevor Farrington, ex-chairman, were both part of the club at this time and couldn't let the opportunity pass without asking the former professional if he would like to lead some training sessions. Over the course of one summer, Tommy put on some sessions for the local players and it understandably went down very well.

Eric Grundy was also playing for the club. He already had a close friendship with Tommy, leading to the latter giving awards out at end-of-season parties and having a connection with Daten, without ever being especially hands-on. That was until Trevor Farrington, the second team's player-manager, was hit with a goalkeeping injury crisis:

I was centre-back and Tommy's son Stephen was playing in the team too. We must have been five or six games before the end of the season and our goalkeeper got injured. We didn't really have cover, we only had two teams back then. So, we didn't really have a proper back-up goalkeeper. I stuck my tongue firmly in my cheek and said to Tom, 'You won't mind a few games between now and the end of the season, would you?'

He was close to being in his 50s and he had long since packed in. He agreed though, and that weekend was his first match. We went to a team called Moore United and their football pitch was at the top of a bit of a climb. It was basically not much more than a cow field, it wasn't very good. Their dressing room was an old portacabin with chicken wire covering the windows because of vandals. There was one shower head for the whole team. We rocked up for Tommy's first game and he walked into the dressing rooms. I know he was very quiet but he chucked his bag in the corner and I can remember it to this day. He said, 'Fucking hell, Trev, fucking San Siro Stadium to this! This is what I've been reduced to!'

He had everyone in stitches. So, we got changed and went out on to the pitch. Moore is near Runcorn, which is on the outskirts of Liverpool, so he was immediately recognised by their team. Their centre-forward must have decided that he was going to make a name for himself. The ball was put over the heads of the defenders and it was running through to the goal area and Tommy came to the edge of the box but the ball wasn't quite going fast enough to carry through to him to pick up. Rather than come out and kick it, he was waiting for the ball to come into the box and then he could pick it up. But this centre-forward came in and clattered him, just as Tommy is waiting for the ball to come in. This bloke just comes in, studs flying and takes Tommy to the cleaners. Of course the ref stops the game. Magic sponge and a bucket of cold water was all we had but Tommy never flinched, never got agitated or angry. He was dead quiet. Didn't give the referee any grief. Didn't give anybody any reason to suspect that at some point he was going to get his revenge.

So, we were at midway through the second half, maybe 40 or 50 minutes after the first incident. They had a corner and the ball came into the box. Tommy came out and punched it so hard, it flew to the halfway line. I'm captain and I'm shouting, 'Right, out lads!' We all run out. I turn round and there's this centre-forward, lying unconscious on the floor. It turns out as Tommy punched the ball with one hand, he'd given this man an upper cut under his jaw with the other and now he's on the floor, absolutely

> out cold. Nobody has seen anything, of course. He finally gets up and Tommy just went over and said, 'You won't do that again, will you?'

After such a long time without playing, it was clear Tommy hadn't lost his winning spirit! This was his first taste of amateur football in the Warrington and District Football League and surprisingly it didn't put him off. He impressed everyone, not just with his obvious talent but in the organisation of his defence and his ability to help coach and manage the matches he took part in. Despite being such a quiet man, he wasn't afraid to bark orders at his defence. It was clear he loved the dressing-room camaraderie once more and it brought the (sometimes slightly violent) best out of him again. There were several instances of opponents trying to be the hero at amateur level but the 'Sweeper Keeper' knew how to handle himself and them. For around 18 months he was part of the club, playing, training and coaching on a semi-regular basis, but this ended swiftly with a move to Warrington.

He would return to Daten to watch his two grandsons, Adam and Scott, when they joined the club. Three generations of Lawrence lads represented Daten and they too hold the proud record of being the venue where Tommy Lawrence played his final competitive match. If anyone looks hard enough, there's probably still a few teeth remaining from the striker that tried to cross him too!

Life after Football

AFTER A footballer has played their final match, things can go in a variety of directions. They can leap into a life of management, where things either skyrocket, as with Bill Shankly, or quickly fizzle out, as in the case of Ron Yeats. Some, more commonly in the modern era, change their kit for a suit and sit in a television studio, where they forget any mistake they ever made while pointing the fingers at those who have taken their place on the grass. Some go into coaching, some change career altogether, while others slip away into the background.

Tommy, other than helping out at Daten, never got involved in management and coaching. Instead, much like many others of his time and in the previous era, he returned to work. He took an ordinary job in a wire factory in Warrington and for many years slipped out of the consciousness of football and the limelight. The failure to be rewarded with a testimonial, though, was to have catastrophic repercussions in his personal life, where he was soon set to literally lose everything.

If we look at his old friend Roger Hunt, the presence of a successful family business with the haulage company meant that he could continue making money and had a stable job in which to do so. Add to that the fame and success of his time at Liverpool, winning the World Cup with England and his testimonial, which provided him the funds to outright buy a new house in a salubrious area of Culcheth, and life was good. Tommy wasn't afforded this, and his pride meant that he never asked for this much-needed match and later never asked for financial help when everything slowly circled out of control.

Many think that Tommy's career ended, everything went well, he appeared on the BBC for his interview in later life and then peacefully passed away. This chapter may be one of the most interesting and surprising though.

* * *

Working life entailed becoming a galvaniser at Rylands, a wire factory in Warrington. His son Steve shared more about his time there: 'He got a job at Rylands and made a lot of good friends, and he enjoyed it. He used to talk about Rylands a lot because he was in the wire manufacturing side of things. He'd talk about the bridges that were built in Japan and he was quite proud of it all. He enjoyed it. He never felt like he had taken a step back.'

The retired goalkeeper also helped work on the roads, toiling in the early hours to help lay the M62. This soon turned to a few pints afterwards and a return to Tommy's house for tales of his playing days and the subsequent dishing out of more priceless memorabilia to anyone who wanted any. A bag of chips, a few pints and an angry wife when she returned home from her nursing job.

Rylands was his main source of income, though, and a place where he worked up to his retirement, making new friends but never to the calibre of those he had met on the football pitch. It's remarkable to think of it now, that someone who had played such a crucial part in a historic period of Liverpool's history was working a normal job. Willie Stevenson moved to Macclesfield and worked in pubs, and was behind the bar at The Kings Head for 20 years. He described life after Anfield: 'I think if you get past the first couple of years, you've got a chance, because in the first couple of years you could end up in the pub and just get pissed! If you're lucky enough, you have got some decent friends and I had one or two. They looked after me and I looked after them.' This was normal life. It wasn't easy adjusting to normality after football, however, and some found it much harder than others.

There was obviously still a keen interest in football. Get-togethers with former players for events and functions was often the only time the whole group socialised together again, but it was immediately comfortable shifting back into the old days. This strong friendship that was built in the 1960s could be rekindled in an instant. It wasn't just Tommy who felt the lack of support from the club, it's commonplace to speak to any member of this team (even those who were given a testimonial) and palpably feel that they were let down by Liverpool in later life. Tracey shared the family's view:

> I know he was always a bit bitter, well my mum was more so than him, about not getting the testimonial. They didn't do anything for him. He was an honorary member at the club but then apparently when he left, they just said, 'You're not an honorary member anymore.' He was thrown on the scrap heap. For a few years there was no Legends Lounge or anything like that, no way for him to go and watch, nothing.

This certainly isn't an isolated incident; Phil Boersma added:

> We used to get two complimentary tickets if we were going to the game but they've been knocked on the head now. It's fucking ridiculous. I find it absolutely incredible that ex-players can't be allowed to get two tickets to go to a game. There was one incident when they gave Tommy one ticket. He was an elderly man, so he'd have to drive all the way on his own. They don't give a fuck about us, it's terrible. What they do for the ex-players is miserable, embarrassing really.

> I don't talk about them, people talk to me about Liverpool. I can't talk about them, because I've got nothing nice to say about them now.

For former players to grow a distaste for the club is saddening insight into a lack of awareness of how much these men still loved the club. To offer an aged former player one ticket, knowing he would have to travel alone and drive in the dark, something he was scared of doing at that point and not really up to after hip and knee replacements, really is showing a huge lack of understanding and empathy. Tommy had to reach out to supporters' groups to help him get to the match, something the club should have arranged themselves. In addition, as the money grew exponentially within the game, Tommy's generation was not only one that put Liverpool in a place from which they could build to being the best team in Europe, but they were also one of the final generations the club would ever need to financially support.

As Howard Gayle said: 'I call that generation "the gods", those that played under Shankly.' They're certainly not treated like it though. The Scouser and former Liverpool player continued:

> I joined Liverpool when I was 19, in 1978. Tommy was obviously retired then but he was coming to the games and I would see him around the ground. The

first time I got to meet him, it was an unbelievable experience for me, with all of that generation. They were my heroes and they gave me so much in the things that they achieved and I call them the beginning of where we are today. To get the chance to shake hands with him and talk with him was amazing. He was so humble and he's looking at me as if to say, 'You're the man.' No, that's you! But what a lovely man.

There were a lot of players who weren't afforded that gratuity of being looked after. Those who were struggling, I don't think that the club did enough for them then and I don't think the club does enough for them today. You see players nowadays, they're going to retire millionaires and it won't be needed in 40–50 years' time. You go and see players who have won everything and they're not living in a massive house, they haven't got loads of money. It doesn't seem right if you see the players' wages today.

Tommy wasn't just any player either. He was really good and he was really agile as a goalkeeper. That was in the day then when he didn't wear gloves too. If you see a lot of Tommy's games, he didn't have gloves on. The modern-day goalkeepers now have got pillows on their hands, haven't they. Imagine having to save one of them heavy balls and the stinging that he must have felt. There was no padding in their

> shirts. The goalkeeping shirts now are like sheepskin coats. In his era it was just a plain green shirt. No tracksuit bottoms, anything like that. Sometimes, when Liverpool would dominate games, you would kind of feel for him because you'd see him running across the box trying to keep himself warm. Then you'd be thinking, *Oh, I hope nobody shoots!*

Tommy was a legendary figure from a legendary era but he was cast aside much like many of his peers. Thankfully a love for Anfield would return once Tracey had managed to help organise the origins of the former players' committee. The likes of Ian Callaghan and Brian Hall were on board and this slowly grew over the years. From Christmas get-togethers where fans could attend, it grew to a level where the club finally started to pay attention and make an effort to facilitate the ex-players, allowing them to reunite, reminisce and share moments with the supporters who loved them. The opportunity for some of the players who had fallen on hard times to recoup some money from these appearances made it worthwhile for everyone, and finally some form of thanks for their years of dedicated service. Tommy's son Steve said that his dad 'fell out of love with the game', but fortunately this love was rekindled when players started to be treated better.

George Scott recalled one day in 2016 when Liverpool dramatically beat Norwich City 5-4. He, Gordon Wallace and Tommy were at an event and were watching it with fans, before engaging in a Q&A afterwards:

> We're sitting there and it was bad news, we were losing and the atmosphere was not brilliant. Tommy said, 'I don't fancy this.' The next minute, Adam Lallana scores the winner, jumps into Jürgen Klopp's arms and we're all celebrating. Tommy says, 'I fancy it now!' I remember saying, 'Look how much it means to him, Tommy.' That was the last time I saw him but his love for Liverpool then was clear.

There was also some after-dinner speaking, where, despite his quiet nature, Tommy knew how to work a crowd with his storytelling ability. Accents for all the players, retelling the lost plinth from the FA Cup Final and countless other comical tales. For one of the best stories that hasn't yet been told, here's George Scott's version:

> Tommy was playing for the reserves and Shankly was watching us. The ball came in and it went through Tommy's legs, over the mud and, by the time he turned round to grab it, it was over the line. We come in at half-time and Tommy is sitting in the dressing room. He knows Shanks is going to come up and talk to him about it, and his head is down. He just

> sees Shankly's shoes coming up and he wants to get in first. So, he says, 'I know, I know, boss, you don't have to tell me. I know I should have kept my legs closed.' Shankly says, 'No, your bloody mother should have kept her legs closed!'

There were some meetings away from the attention of supporters. A picture hangs proudly on the wall in Willie Stevenson's house of all the 1965 squad reuniting many years after their playing days. It was in Southport for Geoff Strong's birthday. They all got on so well and enjoyed a few pints, talking about the good old days.

As time went by and contact became less frequent, sadly the meeting of these old friends seemed to focus around funerals. Although an unhappy day, they always allowed Tommy the chance to bump into a few old faces and share memories once more. If he saw any fringe players on the periphery, he would ensure they were part of the group and introduce everyone – both Jack Whitham and Stan Boardman shared similar stories of him doing this. The overwhelming message from anyone who hadn't seen their former goalkeeper in many years was that it was just like the old days as soon as they met.

One friend in football who unsurprisingly stayed in touch was Roger Hunt. Although the pair were just friends, it really did become a family-like bond. Even today, after the pair have both passed away, their children are still in touch and a family party can't pass for a Lawrence or Hunt without inviting the other family. The pair are so inextricably linked that they're still together long after their passing.

Their love of golf was an easy reason for the duo to stay in touch. Tommy got his handicap down to as low as two, such was the frequency they played. George Scott recalled a time when he and Gordon Wallace played against the two old friends at Leigh Golf Club:

> We went up there to play with them and Tommy was wangling his handicap. He was trying to tell us he was a 24 handicap, and Roger was almost as bad. They were both saying they were a lot worse than they actually were. We said, 'We'll play you for a pound,' so that we didn't lose too much money!
>
> They agreed, first team against the reserves, just like in the old days. We played the round and we ended up beating them on the 18th hole. We all then get into the clubhouse and we're sitting there having a chat about the old days, telling a few Shankly stories, and then it was time to go. I said, 'I've got to go then,' and I got up. Roger went to go, Tommy went to go too, then Gordon says, 'Hey, Roger, what about the pound?'

> Roger said, 'Bloody hell, he might have a Welsh accent but he's a bloody Scotsman, just like you, George!' He threw the pound across, I caught it in my hand and I said, 'It's not every day you get a pound off a World Cup winner, Roger!' That pound is still in my trophy cabinet, it's still there. I've got a picture from that day and Tommy was great that day too.

Gordon Wallace added:

> The two of them talking about all the success these lads had in their careers. Yet they were so humble. We were just the reserves really. We'd all retired but we used to ring up and say, 'Fancy a game of golf?' They would say, 'Love to, no problems.' There's no, 'Oh god, its Gordon Wallace and George Scott again!' Sometimes they would call us and that's a Scottish international goalkeeper ringing us for a game of golf!

Even in the very final days of Tommy's life, Roger was by his side. He visited him in hospital, where the pair would share stories of the good old days. So many years from their crowning glory together at Wembley, but reeling off memories as if it had happened yesterday. From going to the same school, playing for the same youth team, playing for Liverpool together, both staying in Culcheth, playing golf and just remaining friends for life – it truly was a bond for the ages.

* * *

When we last left Tommy in his off-field life, he was part of a community that was blessed with two superstars but left relatively unbothered. As much as spending afternoons in The Pack Horse was a favourite pastime, he was a devoted father to his three children and husband to Judy. His daughter Tracey recalled trips to the swimming baths, to Southport beach and Chester Zoo, where he would take the children and their friends. He loved being the provider, not just to his children but to everyone. If Tracey was taken out dress shopping, he would buy one for her friends too.

This desire to please everyone meant that when autograph hunters came to the door, they would be invited into the house – much to the frustration of his wife! Trips to the cinema were delayed by hordes of people wanting his signature. Nobody was rejected, and one time the start of *Bedknobs and Broomsticks* was missed, much to the frustration of his daughter! It was always a conscious decision to make an effort with everyone but this often bleeds into time with loved ones too. Tommy just never wanted to let anyone down though. Trips to Ayr to see relatives and Norfolk with the Grundy family often filled a summer. This also provided a break from some of the attention, but there's Scousers and

Liverpool fans no matter where you go! There was always a strong bond and connection to Scotland for Tommy, though, and he was incredibly proud to be a Scot.

He would make an effort to be fun, to be happy and everyone loved spending time with him, but he was still spending money like a professional footballer. They were far from living in a mansion but the Lawrence family never had to worry about watching the pennies for their weekly shopping. The family home was a bungalow, but an extension was added during the pomp of his Liverpool career, when he was earning £30 per week (subsidised by the secret ticket sales!). When his time at Liverpool came to an end, Tracey said, 'My dad's mental health must have been struggling.'

Although Tranmere and Chorley still scratched an itch too, as soon as all this ended Tommy came down to earth with a cataclysmic bang. There was nothing in place to ease the transition from performing in front of tens of thousands twice a week to nothing. There was a coaching offer from Bolton where playing could have continued but it never materialised and football just ground to a sudden halt. As his grandson Ryan said, 'He was living a footballer's lifestyle without the paycheck to back it up. These are the issues that are attached from being put into superstardom when you're not really that kind of outgoing person who has had a lot of life experience, because he was so young when he started playing.'

His wife would say that Tommy had three homes, The Pack Horse, the bookies and the family home. It was an unhealthy cycle that was no longer being broken up by playing football and training. His gambling didn't seem out of control, but sitting drinking in a pub all day was a much more normal part of society, especially in a small village. Yet neither are habits that are going to help someone's mental health after losing the buzz and training for and playing professional sport. As much as Tommy was a drinker, he wasn't a drunk. It was a social thing rather than a dependence on alcohol. All this was added to by the sudden death of his mother in 1970, when she and Tommy's father were on holiday in Scotland. A close relationship was lost right at the time he was slipping out of first-team football at the top of the game, which no doubt had a huge effect on him too.

Combine declining mental health, loss of a footballer's wage, an over-reliance on vices such as drinking and gambling to restore a former high of competing at the highest level, and the outcome is no surprise. Always wanting to be, as his son Steve said, 'Mr Popular' was all well and good when he could afford it. Now he was still buying the drinks and putting the bets on but with much less income to support this. By 1976, Tommy's relationship with Judy was on the rocks. Growing frustration between the pair led to bickering on a regular basis. Lots of the smaller details would have occurred behind closed doors and away from the children, but an emotional

Tracey shared the specifics of one evening that changed their family forever:

> They didn't get on very well towards the end. One night, I remember, I don't know why I got up out of bed but my dad was outside. He was really upset, and I never, ever saw my dad upset. I said, 'Why are you upset?' He said, 'Because you're leaving me next week.'
>
> Now, I thought, *You're leaving me next week?* and I just said, 'No, no we're not,' but he must have known the house was going to be repossessed. Then, that was it, he just disappeared for a bit. His mental health must have been terrible at that time. I just remember that time because I had never seen my dad cry. He must have known what was happening and could foresee it all. I couldn't understand it at the time. I was saying, 'What are you on about? We're not leaving, we're not leaving, we're not going anywhere.'

Things had swiftly spiralled out of control. Money had become a major issue and the debt had been cranked up. Tommy's son Steve said, 'I think it was all gambling debt, that's what it was and he had to sell the house to pay off his debts.' The finer details will remain private but it was clear that Tommy hadn't been able to cope with his fall from grace. Much like he had hidden drinking and smoking from his team-mates at Anfield, he was hiding other parts of his life now. There wasn't any violence or infidelity, just two people who grew apart. Add to that the financial concerns that had clearly got so bad that the family home was being repossessed, it was no surprise to see that Judy and the children go one way and Tommy the other.

Tommy went to live with friends and began sofa-surfing as he desperately tried to get his life and finances back on track – while remaining too proud to reveal how bad his situation really was. Judy and the children moved opposite their old home. Luckily the community of Culcheth was so close that friends weren't far away but the pain of watching as their family home was torn apart was almost too much to bear. The lifestyle of a footballer in the 1960s wasn't particularly lavish but it was too much to continue that lifestyle on a basic salary. Just imagine the difference that a well-earned and promised testimonial would have made.

There was a feeling of being let down as Tommy took a large step back from family life. Steve said, 'We didn't see him for six weeks. I don't think we wanted to see him, really. I felt a little bit let down by him. He started working again and we got to see him because he still paid maintenance. We ended up having to go and meet him from his work, then he would give us the money to give to our mum for us.'

He always ensured that he saw the children every weekend, taking them to the cinema or for long walks.

He and Judy stayed amicable for the kids but there was an understandable breakdown in trust and communication. Fortunately, the children could soon move into their own home with their mother and things got back on track for them, but Tommy was seemingly still riddled with debts, even after the house was repossessed.

A move to Warrington soon followed, and rather swiftly and secretly a new woman was on the scene and a second marriage took place. Tommy's children weren't even aware that the wedding had occurred until they saw it in the *Warrington Guardian*. So Tommy began to build a new life for himself, but things had become a lot worse than the family had realised.

Just about everyone has a family and the inevitable difficult family relationships, and this is certainly what occurred in the latter years of Tommy's life. The bridge between crying outside his beloved family home in Culcheth and setting up a new life in Warrington is one that it wasn't fully possible to build for this book. The breakdown of relationships and the family disputes has made the ending to this story rather difficult to share in a fully balanced and fair way. However, Tommy's second marriage helped lift him out of the lowest low of his life, and one person who was able to shed some light on this was his stepson Dale:

> Tommy turned up in my life when I was about 13. He wasn't my stepdad, as a stepdad should be, he was

my mate. He turned out to be one of my best mates. When I got to about 17, he helped me to buy my first car, which was £200. Then he spent another £200 on buying me a new engine for my third car. I've got really good memories about him taking me to Anfield and going into the Legends Lounge quite frequently and meeting dozens of players. He got me into golf too. He took me to buy my first clubs and then took me to Walton Hall golf course, and we used to play regularly before I went to work, at four o'clock in the morning in the summer.

Other really good memories I had was the two times a week I used to go to the pub with my mum, and he was in the darts team. My mum was in the same darts team and Tommy, believe it or not, could not get on the oche unless he had had at least six pints. He was that nervous. He's had fucking 55,000 Kopites at the back of him in the 60s and he couldn't stand on the oche in a pub without having six pints, it's hilarious!

People thought of him as a superstar but he wasn't in my eyes, he was just an okay guy. He was very quiet with people he didn't know, he wouldn't engage in too much chit-chat with people. But if they recognised him for football, he sort of opened up and told them little bits and pieces. The ordinary bloke came out

> of him, finishing his football career and ending up working at Rylands in the wire shop. It's a bit of a comedown. They didn't earn great lots of money them days anyway. He ended up doing an ordinary job in a wire factory in Warrington. He was just a normal bloke.

Asked about how Tommy came into his life, Dale continued:

> I didn't know until later on in life where he ended up. He'd split up with his first wife, all the medals had been sold, he had nothing. I know he ended up in a place called James Lee House. It's run by the Salvation Army in Warrington and basically is a stopover for down-and-outs. He met my mum in a local pub, then the rest is history. I don't recall Tommy struggling for money when he came into my life but I don't know if he was struggling before then, but I do know he was not in a good place where he was living. It's not a nice place.

Tommy treated Dale like a son, like a brother to his three children and they all got on famously too. In particular Dale and Steve were friends and are still in touch today. The pair would go out together in their youth and the relationship they share today is something Tommy would have loved. 'It wasn't a father and son relationship,' Dale added. 'I think it was just two mates, even though I was dead young. When I got older, I think we got stronger, especially going to the match together, having a beer.'

Although Dale didn't view Tommy as a father, it seemed Tommy had other ideas, according to his stepson:

> At the back of my shop, I've got a picture of him in goal. There's posters and things in frames and other stuff. I've got so many books. I've even got a massive book called *This is Anfield* by Steve Hale and Andrew Thompson. Inside, he got all the players to sign it for me on one page and on the other, he wrote, 'To Dale, my son' and then signed it himself. That's my legacy to me, that's what he gave me.

For these pictures, posters and books to still be holding pride of place today shows how important Tommy was to Dale. For the former goalkeeper to write this message shows how much he thought of his stepson too. Both helped each other through a tough time in their lives and the respect they held for each other is clear to see.

* * *

Every effort has been made to ensure that a true reflection of Tommy's life has been told in every sense, and this book has only been written with the best of intentions of sharing the story of one of Liverpool's greatest goalkeepers. Everyone has tough periods and everyone has parts of their life they don't want to share. While it was frustrating to not be able to reveal more about this time, it's not always possible to do so.

If we go on from Tommy's new life and new wife in Warrington, he certainly managed to pick himself up from the unimaginable torture that he had put himself through, and he got his life back on track as a loving father, grandfather and friend. It's important to note that it seemed that Tommy, within ten years of retiring, spent a period of time homeless. This a man who had won the biggest prizes in football, but a lack of financial support after his career meant everything fell apart. Too proud to speak to his friends who would have supported him, he turned to accommodation that was on offer for someone with nowhere else to go. His fighting spirit got him out of that hole, though, and he rebuilt his life.

Known as 'Grandad Football', it was clear that Tommy's legacy was what he had achieved on a football pitch, and he acted as an inspiration to everyone fortunate enough to have him as part of their family life. Taking his grandkids to play football and watching them thrive in their respective teams was the biggest thrill. He stood on the sidelines, supporting his family all year round, often quietly criticising the opposition goalkeeper too! His grandson Ryan recalled: 'I used to get really annoyed. We used to play football against him and he would be in goal but obviously he's an old man and my brother would score a goal past him. I'd go crazy at him, expecting him to still be on this incredible pedestal. In reality, he would come back at me and say, "Do you know how many knees I've had replaced!"'

Although none of his family went on to the heights of Tommy, his son Steve played to a decent level as a goalscoring winger with Warrington Town and Stockport County, and he's now working as a scout for Manchester City. Steve's two sons Adam and Scott are centre-halves, playing to a decent standard, both semi-professional and being paid to play, with Adam receiving a call-up at Scotland Under-17 level. One match against City of Liverpool saw Tommy mobbed by Liverpool fans as he tried to watch on and support his grandsons on the opposite team! Tracey's son Ryan played futsal to such a level that he was invited to train with the Scottish national team – as a goalkeeper. His brother Aaron played in goal too, for a team in Germany, and trained with Carlisle United. Tracey also fancied herself as half decent during her days of playing on the streets with the boys. Perhaps a different era could have opened the door for another Scotland international! Clearly, the love for football and Scotland is still very much in the Lawrence blood.

Even when great-grandchildren came along, Tommy's name of 'Great-Grandad Football' lived on – another nickname to add to the ever-growing list! It seemed he relived his youth vicariously through the grandkids. There were family trips to the bowling alley, where Tommy's winning mentality could always shine through once again. These would often be followed by a tale or two about his days representing Shankly's team. The stories weren't just for the younger generation though; his sister Mary remembers him vividly recalling the sea cadet days of his youth and travelling to London. Stories of the underground were relayed so clearly that it felt as if you were in the capital with him. Tales of his playing days led to showing off whatever medals and memorabilia he had left. He wasn't just generous with his stories but his possessions too, leading to many pieces being given away on a whim. Tracey recalled how his physical memories of his playing days were kept:

> We had a cabinet with all his medals in. He built his own fireplace, my dad, it was proper 70s. It went along the wall and had shelving on top and all his trinkets. But he used to give most of it away. That's the type of person he was.
>
> He gave one of his Scotland caps to a family in Culcheth, he gave another of his friends, Roy Leatherbarrow, the tracksuit from when he ran on the pitch for the 1965 FA Cup Final. His shirt from the game ended up with this man and it was found in his loft when he died. His son, luckily, gave it back to us!

He'd give stuff away when he was socialising. He'd say, 'Oh, I've got this shirt, do you want it?' He gave most things away, but he kept all his medals. We've got a couple of shirts and the tankard from the 1966 Cup Winners' Cup Final. That's in the Anfield museum now. Everything's just been passed around and we'd love to find it all again!

The big mystery is the 1965 FA Cup winner's medal. It went missing and was never found. My dad didn't know where it was. He gave it to his dad, and when he passed away no one could find it – that medal is somewhere! My grandad would not have sold it. We're worried it got buried in the garden and it's still there!

He would give everything away, though, because he knew it would mean something to somebody. If he was in the pub, he would buy everybody a drink, he wanted to treat everybody. That's just the type of person, he was generous to a fault.

Brad Heenan, the son of a heating engineer in Culcheth, recalled going to jobs in both Tommy and Roger Hunt's houses with his dad:

One day my dad said, 'I've got a job here down Culcheth Hall Drive with Roger Hunt. He plays for Liverpool, fantastic player, plays for England and everything. Come with me to this one.'

So me and my brother went, and when the job was done, we said, 'Can you show us your medals, Roger?' He took us in. He's got this massive cabinet with all these trophies and his caps on, and everything was immaculate. We're looking at it thinking, *This is fantastic.*

Then, only about a week later, my dad got a job at Tommy's house, which was only around the corner. We went again, helped with the job and then said the same to Tommy. He said, 'Yeah, no problem. Come on, lads.' He got us a drink and then he showed us some of his medals. With half of them, though, he would say, 'Oh, I think there's another one here stuffed down the side of the couch. There might be a cap on the other side.'

We were thinking, *These are top trophies and he's got them stuffed down the side of the couch!* His kids were probably playing with them, they were everywhere. We were laughing at how the pair were like chalk and cheese, Tommy and Roger. Even though they played in the same team and whatnot, Roger's collection was immaculate, but Tommy's was just everywhere!

This refusal to understand the grandeur of what he was freely giving away speaks of how generous and humble Tommy was. He was happy with sausage and mash, followed by a few pints and then a quiet night at home. All these things were just that – things. This was probably as much just part of the ethos of this team, as Willie Stevenson said: 'You don't have to have the medal to know you won it!' Moments of his career, yes, but they were also just secondary to what he wanted to do in later life. Tommy would head to parties and take things with him, as he knew they meant so much to others and he just wanted to make them happy. A simple man, with simple pleasures, and so modest that he didn't even seem to realise the magnitude of what he had achieved for Liverpool during the 1960s.

If this book can be used for some good for the Lawrence family, though, the desire for them to locate the 1965 FA Cup medal is something that should be thrust into the limelight again. For the family to not even know where it is … that's a huge shame. There's also a wandering Charity Shield medal that pops up on auction sites from time to time too. Although Tommy was happy to give his memories away, there's so many members of his family today that would love to be reunited with them. If anyone has any information, please let them know.

* * *

Sadly, many of these tales come to the same ending. As with many other footballers of this era, dementia had a role to play in the final stages of Tommy's life. Although he wasn't heading the excessively heavy leather balls on cold and wet winter afternoons, his body had been through so much. You don't become known as the first sweeper keeper for being a shrinking violet on your goal line. 'The Flying Pig' threw himself in the way of balls, elbows, boots and anything else bearing down on him and his goal. This clearly seemed to have had an effect; an early example was Tommy's struggles and nerves around driving. This led to his driving licence being revoked and a loss of independence. Dale recalled when this all came to light:

> I ended up taking his car keys off him because he'd gone to the petrol station and he said he'd been driving around for 20 minutes. Driving round and round the pumps because he couldn't get the petrol flap on the right side. I sat him down and said, 'Sit down there, I'll make a coffee.' I said, 'Can I have your keys? Don't worry, I don't want to upset you, but you're not driving anymore, mate, are you?'
>
> You know what he said? He said, 'Thank fuck for that! Two months ago I had to drive to Anfield for a meeting in the middle of winter and it was drizzling. I couldn't see anything, I was so

confused. I didn't know what motorway I was on or anything.'

If I'd have done the wrong thing by taking the keys off him, it would have been a big argument. His reaction showed it was the right thing to do.

It's certainly no coincidence that so many other members of that 1965 FA Cup-winning team succumbed to dementia of some form and it's beyond obvious that there's a link between playing football in that era and having this terrible illness in later life. Despite this struggle with his memory, though, it fortunately didn't grow much worse, but that was because of leukaemia. It was discovered that Tommy had this blood cancer, while dementia was creeping in further. His confusion meant that he never really understood the diagnosis, but within a year he would pass away. Hospital visits for blood transfusions became frequent, which led to one funny moment that was shared by Tracey:

I used to take my dad to the hospital to have blood transfusions and I remember he used to have the nurses in stitches. They wouldn't let him leave one day until he could walk. They said, 'You need to walk down this ward, Tommy, and walk back.' He said, 'What, just walk?' 'Yeah,' they said.

> He goes, 'I'm going to walk down this ward like footballers of today walk.' He was doing this dead shabby walk down the corridor. Then he said, 'And now I'm going to walk back like the real footballers walk,' and he did this posh walk. He had the doctors and nurses in stitches!

Tommy was asked by Peter Hooton to attend the premiere of Mike Todd's film *Shankly: Nature's Fire* in October 2017 and, while he was far from in great health, this fortunately provided a final opportunity to rub shoulders with Ian Callaghan, Tommy Smith and a few other former team-mates. Despite his terrible health, Tommy sat through and wistfully smiled as his old boss spoke to him one more time.

Thanks to the famous BBC interview and the passing of time that held Shankly's first team in such high regard, Tommy was known as a Liverpool legend. The opportunity for any fan to see him was something that had to be capitalised upon, and his newfound fame because of his viral video meant that a younger generation wanted to speak to him too. As he stood outside the Liverpool Philharmonic waiting to be picked up, he was mobbed by supporters who were delighted to see their former hero once again. Tracey compared it to how it would have been if Patrick Swayze was spotted outside the premiere of *Dirty Dancing*. Little did they all know that in under three months the great man's story would come to an end.

Trips to the hospital for blood transfusions became more frequent and, as his health quickly deteriorated, it was clear that the end was closing in. It was while Tommy was in Warrington Hospital that grandson Ryan started recording and writing down some of the amazing memories he had taken for granted over the years.

Tommy refused the offer to go to a hospice, so he could be at home among family and friends. He would watch his old cowboy films on TV, in between cups of 'very hot tea'. The likes of Roger Hunt and Bill Bygroves – the club chaplain – visited but it was mainly family by his side. Tommy chatted with his sister Mary about their childhood in Ayr, never failing to impress her with the detail in which he could recall so many different events – all while still making everyone laugh. When Tommy finally slipped away, it was no surprise, and at least it came with the solace that many people had been able to say their goodbyes and that he passed away at home – where he always wanted to be.

Epilogue

TOMMY PASSED away on 10 January 2018. It led to a huge outpouring of love and appreciation, largely for what he had done as a footballer, but everyone agreed upon how great a man he was too. His funeral took place by the end of the month, the coffin draped with a Liverpool-emblazoned banner that read 'Tommy'. His newfound fame and hugely successful career made it headline news once again.

Those present was like a who's who of Liverpool history. The likes of Kenny Dalglish, Ray Clemence, Phil Neal, Willie Stevenson, Kevin Keegan, Roger Hunt and so many others. Younger players such as Howard Gayle and Robbie Fowler attended, which showed how the goalkeeper touched generations other than just his own. It was clear to any younger members of his family just how much Tommy meant to so many influential people. Then there were the cameras and hordes of mourners; this was a day that so many people wanted to ensure they attended. Largely thanks to the growth of the 'Shankly Heroes Nights' that had been held and organised by Tracey and Carol Maloney (Chris Lawler's niece) in an effort to raise awareness that there needed to be a former players' association, there was a real effort made by former team-mates and representatives from Liverpool to attend. 'You'll Never Walk Alone' was played – a fitting tribute to Tommy's contribution to football.

For all that Liverpool FC had failed Tommy in terms of a testimonial and how they treated him after his retirement, at least they did step up in the aftermath of his passing. First came the video *Tommy Lawrence: In His Own Words*, which helped tell the story of his time at Anfield through the voice of the 'Sweeper Keeper'. Not just powerful but an everlasting memory for the family, who can hear his voice with the click of a button today. Then came Liverpool's league match against Manchester City, not only a thriller on the pitch as the Reds ran out 4-3 victors against a previously undefeated opponent that season, but a match that befitted the occasion. It was a poignant homage to a former hero. Tributes filled the programme, a minute's applause preceded kick-off for 'the great Tommy Lawrence', then the Kop broke out into an emotional rendition of 'You'll Never Walk Alone' in his honour. Some tickets were provided for the family but not enough to fill the demand. Fortunately, compassionate supporters gave their tickets to many family members. Although they were dotted around the stadium, it allowed them all a unique perspective of a hugely emotional moment for them all.

Tommy's legacy at the club is that he was the goalkeeper for the era that's widely considered the birth of the modern Liverpool, who would go on to dominate in England and Europe. He held the role with pride, never let anybody down and helped pave the way for Ray Clemence to go on and achieve everything he did in the coming years under Bob Paisley. As well as this, inside the club's new AXA Training Centre there stands a wall that's dedicated to the iconic stoppers in Anfield history. Commissioned by the current goalkeeping coach John Achterberg, it features everyone who's been in goal for any trophy-winning team in the club's history. The wall acts as motivation to the current goalkeepers and details the appearances and trophy wins of each man, meaning Tommy's achievements are used as a daily reminder to the current squad of the heights they need to aspire to.

Add to this the seemingly forever-viral video that just won't go away, and it's certain that Tommy won't be forgotten by Liverpool or by their supporters. It's such a shame that this level of respect wasn't shown during his playing days.

* * *

It's hard to spend so long following the life of one man from start to finish and to summarise or conclude thoughts on it all in a fitting way. Tommy Lawrence came from very humble beginnings and quickly learned about working hard to chase your dreams. Then he watched his life being turned upside down with a huge move south. This couldn't have worked out any better, though, meeting Roger and Peter Hunt and setting himself up in a village that will forever be known as his home.

A realisation of the importance of not forgetting your roots, while striving to become Liverpool's No.1, all coincided with the emergence of a certain Bill Shankly. The manager needed his players and vice versa, but there can't have been many better times for Tommy to try to make a name for himself as a goalkeeper. Yes, the riches and even more silverware would have followed in later years, but his youth, enthusiasm and trailblazing talent meant that coming into a team that had just been promoted from the second tier was perfectly timed.

The achievements between 1964 and 1966 were unparalleled in the club's history and nobody will ever forget the first Liverpool team to win the FA Cup. Years of dedication and foolhardy refusal to give in to injury meant that Tommy was an ever-glowing star in a team of deteriorating talent. On his removal from the team, it's easy to base it all around that one match against Watford, but the way in which he lost his place to Ray Clemence shows that it was more than that. Tommy never let Liverpool down, and his first experience of injury came at a time of a long-awaited decision to change the starting line-up.

This simply opened the door to one of the greatest goalkeepers to ever play the game to take his place, while also beginning a new role for Tommy as a mentor. Passing on everything he knew to a man learning his trade led to a better future for Clemence and Liverpool – to the detriment of Tommy. He was robbed of a much-deserved testimonial by Liverpool, lied to by Tranmere, and let go of by his old friend Ron Yeats. Again though, Tommy's focus was on nothing but helping his replacement thrive in his position.

Chorley followed, and other than Daten it was the end of his playing days. It could all have been so different if things had been put in place for footballers after retirement. The money he missed out on through a lack of a testimonial, his declining mental health, his increasing gambling and drinking, which led to the breakdown of his family – all could have been avoided. But even when at his lowest ebb, the work ethic instilled by his parents and the inability to show that you're down or hurt meant that Tommy fought back. He got back on his feet, became known as a footballer again and just so happened to be walking through Liverpool city centre at the most opportune moment to catapult his life back into the limelight. It probably didn't change his viewpoint on his life too much then, but it meant that, once Tommy passed away in 2018, everyone knew who he was.

Now that his story can be told in much more detail, it's clear to see that it's an oxymoronic life of great fortune and misfortune in equal measures. Born in a different time, he would have lived a very different life. However, if you could offer the young lad moving down from Scotland to Culcheth the opportunity to play 390 times for Liverpool, win the honours he did and receive the adulation from his loyal supporters on the Kop, he would have bitten your hand off!

A life well lived by a man that nobody had a bad word to say about. A pioneer as a goalkeeper, an inspiration as a person, a loving father, grandfather, great-grandfather and friend – and a humble man, despite everything he achieved. There won't be another Tommy Lawrence. This was his story.

Records and Statistics

Team	Season	League			FA Cup			League Cup			Europe			Charity Shield			Total		
		A	CS	GC	A	CS	GC	A	CS	GC	A	CS	GC	A	CS	GC	A	CS	GC
Liverpool	1962/63	29	8	39	6	2	4	-	-	-	-	-	-	-	-	-	**35**	**10**	**43**
Liverpool	1963/64	40	12	43	5	2	3	-	-	-	-	-	-	-	-	-	**45**	**14**	**46**
Liverpool	1964/65	41	6	72	8	5	3	-	-	-	9	5	7	1	0	2	**59**	**16**	**84**
Liverpool	1965/66	42	19	34	1	0	2	-	-	-	9	4	6	1	0	2	**53**	**23**	**44**
Liverpool	1966/67	41	13	46	4	2	2	-	-	-	5	2	10	1	1	0	**51**	**18**	**58**
Liverpool	1967/68	42	10	40	9	3	8	2	0	4	6	2	5	-	-	-	**59**	**15**	**57**
Liverpool	1968/69	42	21	24	4	2	2	2	1	2	2	0	3	-	-	-	**50**	**24**	**31**
Liverpool	1969/70	28	9	30	5	3	2	2	0	4	2	0	3	-	-	-	**37**	**12**	**39**
Liverpool	1970/71	1	0	2	-	-	-	-	-	-	-	-	-	-	-	-	**1**	**0**	**2**
Tranmere	1971/72	35	9	59	7	2	10	-	-	-	-	-	-	-	-	-	**42**	**11**	**69**
Tranmere	1972/73	37	10	39	2	1	2	1	0	1	-	-	-	-	-	-	**40**	**11**	**42**
Tranmere	1973/74	8	2	8	2	0	4	2	1	3	-	-	-	-	-	-	**12**	**3**	**15**
Scotland		3	0	5	-	-	-	-	-	-	-	-	-	-	-	-	**3**	**0**	**5**
Total		**389**	**119**	**441**	**53**	**22**	**42**	**9**	**2**	**14**	**33**	**13**	**34**	**3**	**1**	**4**	**487**	**157**	**535**

* A = Appearances
* CS = Clean Sheets
* GC = Goals Conceded
* Match details for Chorley and Daten not fully available. A, B, C, Reserves and international u23 matches not included

Honours: First Division 1963/64, 1965/66; FA Cup 1965
Charity Shield 1966, 1964 (shared), 1965 (shared); European Cup Winners' Cup 1966 (runners-up); Central League 1969/70, 1970/71; Liverpool Senior Cup 1962; Liverpool Challenge Cup 1959; Lancashire Cup 1962 (runners-up)

Bibliography

Interviews

Mary Bailey
Stan Boardman
Phil Boersma
Ian Callaghan
Roy Evans
Trevor Farrington
Doug Fraser
Howard Gayle
Eric Grundy Jnr
Eric Grundy Snr
Brad Heenan
Mike Henshall
Liz Hoare
David Hunt
Julie Hunt
Dick Johnson
John Kaye
Chris Lawler
Adam Lawrence
Jayne Lawrence
Scott Lawrence
Steve Lawrence
Kevin Lewis
Ray Mathias
Frank McLintock
Gordon Milne
Ryan Murray
Tracey Murray
Dale Roberts
George Scott
Willie Stevenson
Jimmy Tarbuck
Bobby Thomson
Gordon Wallace
Paul White
Jack Whitham

Books

Baldursson, A. & Magnusson, G., *Liverpool: The Complete Record.*

Baldursson, A. & Magnusson, G., *The Liverpool Encyclopaedia.*

Ball, A., *Alan Ball's International Soccer Annual.*

Barwick, B. & Sinstadt, G., *Everton v Liverpool: A Celebration of the Merseyside Derby.*

Barwick, B. & Sinstadt, G., *The Great Derbies: Everton versus Liverpool.*

Dohren, D., *Ghost on the Wall: The Authorised Biography of Roy Evans.*

Historic Newspapers Ltd., *Liverpool Headlines from 1906: A Newspaper History.*

Jones, P.K., *Crossing the Park: The Men Who Dared to Play for Both Liverpool & Everton.*

Jones, P.K., *Liddell at One Hundred: A Family Portrait of a Liverpool Icon.*

Kelly, S.F., *Bill Shankly: It's Much More Important Than That.*

Kelly, S.F., *Liverpool: The Official Illustrated History 1892–1995.*

Liversedge, S., *Liverpool: The Official Centenary History.*

Marsden, A., *Liverpool Football Programmes.*

Platt, M., *120 Men Who Made LFC.*

Ponting, I., *Liverpool: Player by Player.*

Ponting, I. & Hale, S., *Sir Roger: The Life and Times of Roger Hunt, A Liverpool Legend.*

Rowlands, G.A., *The Red Men of Liverpool Football Club.*

Shankly, B., *Shankly: My Story: The Autobiography. Unique 50th Anniversary Edition.*

St John, I., *The Saint: My Autobiography.*

Walmsley, D. & Done, S., *The History of Liverpool FC.*

Williams, J., *Red Men: Liverpool Football Club: The Biography.*

Websites

BritishNewspaperArchive.co.uk
LFChistory.net, Arnie Baldursson and Gudmundur Magnusson
PlayUpLiverpool.com, Kjell Hanssen

Other

Liverpool FC Official Matchday Programmes, author's own collection

Index